2024 Edititon

AI FOR BEGINNERS

The Ultimate Guide to Mastering Generative Intelligence, From Theory to Practice

ALAN MILLER

© Copyright 2023 – Alan Miller- All rights reserved.

The content contained within this book may not be reproduced, duplicated or transmitted without direct written permission from the author or the publisher.

Under no circumstances will any blame or legal responsibility be held against the publisher, or author, for any damages, reparation, or monetary loss due to the information contained within this book. Either directly or indirectly.

Legal Notice:

This book is copyright protected. This book is only for personal use. You cannot amend, distribute, sell, use, quote or paraphrase any part, or the content within this book, without the consent of the author or publisher.

Disclaimer Notice:

Please note the information contained within this document is for educational and entertainment purposes only. All effort has been executed to present accurate, up to date, and reliable, complete information. No warranties of any kind are declared or implied. Readers acknowledge that the author is not engaging in the rendering of legal, financial, medical or professional advice. The content within this book has been derived from various sources. Please consult a licensed professional before attempting any techniques outlined in this book. By reading this document, the reader agrees that under no circumstances is the author responsible for any losses, direct or indirect, which are incurred as a result of the use of information contained within this document, including, but not limited to, — errors, omissions, or inaccuracies.

- **INTRODUCTION TO ARTIFICIAL INTELLIGENCE** 7
  - WHAT IS ARTIFICIAL INTELLIGENCE? 7
  - THE HISTORY OF ARTIFICIAL INTELLIGENCE: A SPIRITED TIMELINE 9
  - THE IMPORTANCE OF AI 10
- **FOUNDATIONS OF AI** 13
  - BASIC TERMINOLOGY AND CONCEPTS 13
  - TYPES OF AI: NARROW AI VS. GENERAL AI 15
- **INTRODUCTION TO GENERATIVE AI** 20
  - WHAT IS GENERATIVE AI? 20
- **DIVING DEEPER INTO AI AND GENERATIVE AI** 25
  - DATA: THE FUEL OF AI 25
  - DATA COLLECTION: THE CHOREOGRAPHY 26
  - COMPUTING POWER: THE MUSCLE BEHIND AI 29
  - MACHINE LEARNING BASICS 34
- **DEEP LEARNING AND NEURAL NETWORKS** 40
  - WHAT ARE NEURAL NETWORKS? 40
- **APPLICATIONS OF GENERATIVE AI** 45
  - GENERATIVE AI IN ART AND CREATIVITY: UNVEILING NEW DIMENSIONS 45
  - GENERATIVE AI IN BUSINESS AND MARKETING 49
  - GENERATIVE AI IN SCIENTIFIC RESEARCH AND INNOVATIONS 54
  - TEXT GENERATION WITH AI 60
  - IMAGE GENERATION WITH AI 80
  - VIDEO GENERATION WITH AI 86
  - MUSIC CREATION WITH AI 96
  - DATA ANALYSIS WITH GENERATIVE AI 104

CODING WITH AI 112
CHATGPT IN EVERYDAY LIFE: YOUR AI ASSISTANT 117
   SIMPLIFYING COMMUNICATION 117
   ENHANCING PRODUCTIVITY 117
   LEARNING AND DEVELOPMENT 118
   DAILY DECISION MAKING 118
   PERSONAL WELL-BEING 118
THE CRAFT OF PROMPT ENGINEERING WITH CHATGPT 120
   UNDERSTANDING THE BASICS OF EFFECTIVE PROMPTING 120
   ADVANCED TECHNIQUES IN PROMPT ENGINEERING . 120
   REAL-WORLD APPLICATIONS OF PROMPT ENGINEERING 121
   BEST PRACTICES IN PROMPT ENGINEERING 121
   CUSTOM INSTRUCTIONS IN CHAT GBT 124
FUTURE OF GENERATIVE AI 127
   INCREASED MODEL EFFICIENCY IN GENERATIVE AI ... 128
   INTEGRATION OF MULTIMODAL MODELS IN GENERATIVE AI 129
   ADVANCES IN PERSONALIZATION THROUGH GENERATIVE AI 131
   SOCIETAL IMPACT OF GENERATIVE AI 133
CONCLUSION 137

INTRODUCTION TO ARTIFICIAL INTELLIGENCE
WHAT IS ARTIFICIAL INTELLIGENCE?

Welcome to the world of Artificial Intelligence (AI), where the machines are learning, and no, it's not just to beat you at chess or autocorrect your texts into embarrassment. AI is like that one kid in class who aces the tests without studying—a bit showy, incredibly useful, and slightly unnerving.

So, what is AI? Imagine if you could bottle up a scientist's brain, a detective's intuition, and a cat's ability to ignore you—all in one computer program. That's AI. It's dedicated to solving problems that typically require human brains, like understanding this sentence or figuring out how to win a game of Go without flipping the board.

AI operates on a principle that's both inspiring and slightly insulting: that human smarts can be boiled down to something so precise even a machine could do it. And not just do it, but maybe do it better. The nerve, right? Researchers are hustling to make machines think like us, learn like us, and understand like us, though they haven't yet cracked making them binge-watch TV shows like us.

As we dive headfirst into this rabbit hole, we'll look at AI's party tricks. There's the Narrow AI, like those chatbots that apologize a lot but don't always fix your problems, and General AI, the big dream where machines will be our intellectual plus-ones, helping us solve mysteries like where your left sock disappears to after laundry day.

In this joyride through the land of artificial smarts, we'll uncover how these digital Einsteins are changing everything. So, buckle up, and let's get this computational party started. Who knows? By the end of this, you might just be convinced that AI is the best thing since sliced bread—or at least since the bread-slicing machine.

BONUS CONTENT

As a token of appreciation for your support, I'm excited to offer you this exclusive bonus: "Mastering GBTS". This guide dives into the world of Generative Pre-trained Transformers (GPTs), offering you a hands-on approach to understanding and mastering one of today's most innovative AI technologies.

To access the bonus, simply scan the QR code below using your smartphone or tablet. This will take you to a secure download page where you can grab your copies.

In addition, by scanning the QR code below you can get the opportunity to become a part of our exclusive ARC team. As a member, you'll have the chance to receive early releases of new books, provide feedback, and help shape the future publications. This is a wonderful opportunity for avid readers and enthusiasts in the field to engage more deeply with our content and contribute to the community.

And if you will enjoy the book, I would be incredibly grateful if you could leave a review. Your feedback is not just valuable for my understanding of what aspects of the book connected with you, but it also assists others in discovering this book. It plays a crucial role in encouraging both the curious and the skeptical to embark on their own journey into AI exploration.

THE HISTORY OF ARTIFICIAL INTELLIGENCE: A SPIRITED TIMELINE

Prelude to a Digital Mind

The history of AI is like a classic hero's journey, complete with thrilling ups, despondent downs, and a cast of characters who were both geniuses and dreamers. It all started way back when 'computer' was a job title for humans, mainly women, who were calculating war trajectories faster than a room full of high school students could say "When are we ever going to use this in real life?"

The Golden Age: When AI Was an Overachiever

In the 1950s, AI was the new kid on the academic block. The term 'Artificial Intelligence' was the brainchild of John McCarthy and friends at the Dartmouth Conference in 1956, where they predicted AI would be the next big thing. They set the stage for a future where machines would be more than glorified calculators—they'd be thinkers.

The AI Winters: Someone Turn the Heat Back On

Then came the AI winters, the mood swings of the technological world. Funding dried up like a grape in the sun, and skepticism was as common as a '404 Error' page. These were the times when AI's grand promises felt as distant as a Wi-Fi signal in the wilderness.

The Renaissance: AI Gets Its Groove Back

But you can't keep a good idea down for long. By the 1990s, AI was back with more focus and better haircuts. Thanks to the internet and a little something called 'big data', machine learning algorithms were suddenly the cool kids in Silicon Valley. They learned from data like overzealous students, and soon, they were everywhere, from filtering our emails to recommending what song you might like next—often with surprising accuracy.

The Roaring AI Present: Intelligence Everywhere

Now we're in an era where AI is as ubiquitous as a smartphone screen in a teenager's hand. It's driving cars, brewing beer, and writing articles. It's in our pockets, on our wrists, and in our living rooms. Sometimes, it's hard to tell whether AI is a tool, a partner, or that nosy neighbor who knows a little too much about your schedule.

What's Next? The AI of Tomorrow

We stand at the cusp of an AI future that's as unpredictable as a plot twist in a telenovela. Will AI become the best thing since sliced bread, or will it be a reminder to be careful what we wish for? Only time will tell, but one thing is certain: the journey of AI is one of the most fascinating stories of our time, a blend of ambition, innovation, and a dash of old-fashioned human hubris.

THE IMPORTANCE OF AI

In the grand tapestry of modern innovation, Artificial Intelligence (AI) is the golden thread weaving through the fabric of our lives, subtly and profoundly transforming the world as we know it. It's like a Swiss Army knife in our collective pocket—versatile, sometimes inscrutable, and endlessly useful.

AI is the silent engine powering our smartphones, the secret sauce in our favorite apps, and the unseen hand guiding autonomous vehicles. It's our navigator in the complex digital landscape, our shield against cyber threats, and the new paintbrush for creators and artists. This technology is like the industrious bees of our digital ecosystem, buzzing away in the background, essential yet often unnoticed.

In the economic arena, AI is a game-changer. It's an invisible workforce, driving efficiencies that turbocharge industries from manufacturing to finance. With AI, supply chains are becoming more resilient, markets more predictive, and personalization is reaching new heights in retail. It's not just making businesses smarter; it's spawning entirely new business models and reshaping the labor market.

But AI's reach extends beyond commerce into the realm of ethics and society, where it serves as both a beacon of potential and a source of thorny dilemmas. It prompts us to ask profound questions about what it means to be human in an age where machines can learn, create, and even 'understand.' AI is a mirror, reflecting our intelligence and our biases, challenging us to be better stewards of this powerful new tool.

As we stand on the precipice of an AI-driven future, the importance of AI isn't just in how it can optimize a database or predict the weather. It's in its potential to enhance human capabilities, to solve some of our most intractable problems, and to open doors to worlds we've yet to imagine. AI could be our ticket to a sustainable future, where it helps us to combat climate change, manage resources, and forge paths to new frontiers in space and medicine.

We are just beginning to scratch the surface of what AI can do. It's a revolution, a challenge, and an invitation to a dance with technology where humans lead, but AI is quickly learning the steps. With each algorithm and each data set, we're teaching these digital creations how to move in harmony with us, to the rhythm of human progress.

In this book, we'll explore the vast landscape of AI, without hyperbole or fear-mongering, but with a clear-eyed view of its potential and its pitfalls. AI is not the end of the story of human ingenuity—it's a fascinating new chapter, and we're only just turning the first page.

FOUNDATIONS OF AI
BASIC TERMINOLOGY AND CONCEPTS
To kick things off, let's unwrap some basic terms:

Generative AI: This is one of the most exciting frontiers in AI, the realm of creation. Generative AI refers to algorithms that can generate new content, be it text, images, music, or even video, that is similar but not identical to data it has been trained on. It's like an AI artist given a set of past works as inspiration to create something original. From creating new fashion designs to generating realistic human voices, generative AI is pushing the boundaries of what machines can create.

Algorithm: At the core of any AI system is an algorithm, a set of rules or instructions laid down for solving a problem or performing a task. Think of it as the DNA of software, a blueprint that guides the system through the complexities of decision-making. It's not just a single recipe but an entire cookbook, with each algorithm offering a different culinary strategy to turn data ingredients into a feast of insights.

Data: AI thrives on data. This isn't just any old information, but rather high-quality, structured data that machines can digest. It's the fuel for the AI engine, and the quality of this fuel can greatly affect the performance of the system. Data is like the experiences we accumulate throughout our lives; it shapes the AI, informs its decisions, and ultimately determines how well it can mimic human intelligence. Without diverse and comprehensive data, AI would be as effective as a car trying to run on empty.

Machine Learning (ML): Machine Learning is the whiz-kid of AI, the field where computers get a crash course in human ingenuity. It's where algorithms are fed data and then left to figure out the patterns and make predictions. The beauty of ML is its ability to find needles of insight in haystacks of data without human intervention. It's a bit like a self-taught artist who starts with stick figures and progresses to masterpieces through trial and error.

Neural Network: If AI is the brain, then neural networks are the synapses firing away inside it. These are computing systems vaguely inspired by the biological neural networks that constitute animal brains. A neural network is a web of nodes linked together in a way that resembles how neurons interact. This structure allows the system to learn in a more human-like way, adjusting connections based on the flow of data. It's the backbone of most modern AI, giving it the flexibility to learn from complex patterns.

Deep Learning: Deep Learning is the honor student in the AI class, a technique that employs multi-layered neural networks to digest large amounts of data. Imagine like drilling down into the layers of the Earth; each layer captures and processes more abstract features of the data, getting more sophisticated as it goes deeper. Deep Learning is behind some of the most futuristic AI feats, like recognizing faces, translating languages, and driving cars.

Supervised Learning: Imagine a sort of on-the-job training for AI. You give the machine a data set where the "right answers" (outcomes) are included, and it learns to make predictions based on the input data. It's like a teacher guiding a student through a textbook, except the textbook is made of numbers, and the student never needs a lunch break.

Unsupervised Learning: This is where AI gets a bit more adventurous. You let the algorithm loose on data without any predefined answers, and it starts to identify patterns and relationships all on its own. Think of it as a toddler wandering through a toy store, finding all sorts of interesting things without any guidance.

Reinforcement Learning: Here, AI learns by doing. It's like training a dog with treats; the AI takes actions in an environment to achieve some goal, receiving rewards or penalties along the way. It's a trial-and-error process in a simulated environment, and the algorithm learns from past actions to improve its future actions.

Natural Language Processing (NLP): This field is all about giving AI the gift of gab. NLP technologies enable computers to understand, interpret, and generate human language, including the nuances of context. It's what allows AI to write articles, understand tweets, or have a chat with you.

Computer Vision: This is AI's ability to see and understand images and videos. It's teaching computers to interpret and make decisions based on visual data, almost like giving them a pair of electronic eyes. From facial recognition to medical image analysis, computer vision is helping machines understand our world visually.

Cognitive Computing: A subset of AI that attempts to mimic human thought processes in a computerized model. Cognitive computing systems use pattern recognition, data mining, and NLP to mimic the human brain, making decisions that are not just logical, but also reasoned and contextual.

TYPES OF AI: NARROW AI VS. GENERAL AI

In the landscape of Artificial Intelligence, we find two distinct territories: Narrow AI and General AI. Each has its own set of rules, capabilities, and ambitions.

Narrow AI: The Specialist

Narrow AI, also known as Weak AI, is the type of intelligence that's all around us today, specialized in performing specific tasks with intelligence. Imagine a world-class chess player who can outmaneuver any human opponent but can't engage in a simple conversation about the weather. That's Narrow AI—it excels in structured environments with clear rules but doesn't venture beyond its narrow set of skills.

Examples of Narrow AI are plentiful:

Virtual Assistants: Siri, Alexa, and Google Assistant can help you check the weather, set reminders, or play music. They're smart in their domain but ask them to do something outside of their programming, and they're lost.

Recommendation Systems: The algorithms behind Netflix's movie suggestions or Amazon's product recommendations are Narrow AI. They analyze your past behavior to predict what you might like next but can't make judgments about unrelated areas of your life.

Autonomous Vehicles: Self-driving cars use Narrow AI to navigate roads, recognize objects, and make driving decisions, but they can't do much else.

General AI: The Jack of All Trades

General AI, on the other hand, is the broader, more ambitious cousin of Narrow AI. It's the concept of a machine with the ability to apply intelligence across a wide range of tasks, similar to a human being. It's the kind of AI you see in science fiction—the robots and computers that understand and interact with the world in a way indistinguishable from humans.

General AI doesn't exist yet, but it represents the ultimate goal of many AI researchers. It would be a flexible, adaptable intelligence capable of learning how to perform a vast array of tasks, from composing symphonies to conducting complex scientific research.

If we were to see examples of General AI, they might look like this:

A Medical Robot: That can diagnose diseases, perform surgery, conduct psychological counseling, and even engage in bedside manner, adapting to new medical research without needing to be reprogrammed.

An AI Scientist: Capable of developing new theories, conducting experiments, and even understanding the ethical implications of its own work.

The leap from Narrow AI to General AI is vast. It's not just a step up in complexity; it's a fundamental change in capability and versatility. Narrow AI operates within a predefined scope, while General AI requires a level of understanding and adaptability that's currently beyond our reach.

The distinction between Narrow AI and General AI is crucial. It helps us understand the limitations of current AI technologies and the potential for future advancements. It sets the stage for discussions about the implications of AI in our society, the ethics of AI development, and the future of human work. As we continue to push the boundaries of what machines can do, the journey from Narrow AI towards General AI will likely be one of the defining narratives of our technological evolution.

While Narrow AI is like a virtuoso musician, brilliant within a certain repertoire, General AI would be akin to a complete orchestra, capable of playing any piece from any genre, even composing new symphonies on the fly. It's the difference between an expert chess-playing program and a sentient android from a sci-fi novel that can learn to play chess, invent a new game, or choose to write poetry instead.

General AI would not just understand tasks but also contexts and subtleties, the kind of understanding that allows a human to navigate the world's complexities. It would possess something akin to common sense and the ability to transfer knowledge between domains.

In essence, Narrow AI is AI that does, while General AI is AI that understands and innovates. The transition from the current state of Narrow AI to the aspirational General AI involves not just technological advancements but also a deeper conceptual breakthrough, redefining our relationship with machines and our understanding of intelligence itself.

Overview of Machine Learning and Deep Learning

In the grand ballroom of Artificial Intelligence, Machine Learning (ML) and Deep Learning (DL) are the dancers that everyone watches. They've transformed the AI party, bringing new moves that have changed the tempo and rhythm of innovation.

Machine Learning: The Art of Pattern Recognition

Machine Learning is the art and science of getting machines to act without being explicitly programmed. In the past, we had to painstakingly instruct computers on how to do everything. ML changed the game by enabling computers to learn from data, identify patterns, and make decisions with minimal human intervention.

At its heart, ML is about prediction and efficiency. When your email filters spam, when your bank detects fraudulent transactions, or when your favorite streaming service recommends a movie you might like—that's Machine Learning in action. It's the workhorse of Narrow AI, dedicated to specific tasks, and it's incredibly good at them.

Machine Learning operates through several methodologies:

Supervised Learning, where models learn to predict outcomes from labeled data. Unsupervised Learning, which finds hidden patterns or intrinsic structures in input data. Reinforcement Learning, a type of ML where an agent learns to behave in an environment by performing actions and seeing the results.

Deep Learning: Neural Networks at Play

Deep Learning is a subset of ML based on artificial neural networks, and it's one of the primary reasons AI has leapt forward in recent years. If ML is high school, DL is post-grad work. It deals with larger datasets, more complex patterns, and it can learn features directly from the data.

Deep Learning shines in tasks like image and speech recognition, powering systems that can recognize your face or voice with an accuracy that rivals humans. It's the technology behind self-driving cars that navigate traffic, digital assistants that understand your queries, and even in healthcare, where it helps to identify diseases in medical scans.

Deep Learning's success stems from its neural networks, which have layers (hidden layers) between inputs and outputs. These layers can learn increasingly abstract representations of the data. For instance, in image recognition, the first layer might recognize edges, the next layer shapes, and further layers might identify textures or patterns.

Roles in the AI Ecosystem

The roles of ML and DL are akin to that of an expert and a master. ML is the expert, specialized in extracting insights from data, automating tasks, and bringing precision to processes. DL, the master, takes it further by tackling more complex, intuitive tasks that require a deeper understanding and a more sophisticated approach.

Together, Machine Learning and Deep Learning form the backbone of contemporary AI applications. They're not just tools; they are the craftsmen, continuously carving out new possibilities and pushing the boundaries of what machines can do. As we stand on the brink of AI's potential, ML and DL are the forces that will drive us into a future where AI is not just a tool but a partner in every aspect of human endeavor.

INTRODUCTION TO GENERATIVE AI
WHAT IS GENERATIVE AI?

Generative AI is the cool creator of the artificial intelligence family, the one that throws paint on a canvas and calls it an algorithm. It's where AI stops playing games of chess and starts writing the rules for new games. In technical terms, Generative AI refers to algorithms that use machine learning to generate new data that resembles the training data.

Here's the real kicker: it's not just about creating a single output. Generative AI can produce a diverse array of results, each with its own unique flair. It's like a novelist who can write in the style of Hemingway one minute and J.K. Rowling the next. The applications are as varied as they are impressive, from generating photorealistic images to composing music, and even creating synthetic datasets that can be used to train other AI models without the privacy concerns of real data.

How Generative AI Works

To understand how Generative AI works, you might picture it as an AI being apprenticing under a master craftsman, learning to emulate their style. It starts with a model, like a GAN or VAE, studying a dataset until it understands the patterns and structures that make up, say, a face or a piece of music. Then, when it's time to create, the model applies its knowledge to generate new instances that maintain the essence of the original without being mere copies.

With GANs, it's a tug-of-war: the generator creates, the discriminator judges, and with each iteration, the generator gets better at its job. It's like a feedback loop where the AI is constantly refining its art, learning from each critique. On the other hand, VAEs are more introspective. They encode data into a lower-dimensional space and then decode it, adding a little something extra each time to produce results that carry the echo of the original but with a new voice.

Key Technologies Behind Generative AI

The star players in the Generative AI team are GANs and Autoencoders, each bringing a unique approach to the creative process.

Generative Adversarial Networks (GANs): These are the competitive ones, the AIs that thrive on the challenge. The generator network creates outputs, and the discriminator network evaluates them. It's a constant battle of wits, where the generator is trying to sneak a fast one past the discriminator, and with every round, it learns a bit more about how to make its creations more convincing.

Autoencoders: These are the introspective artists of the AI world. They take in data, compress it down to the most critical points, and then reconstruct it. The trick is that during reconstruction, the AI can add its own flair. VAEs, a type of autoencoder with a twist, introduce randomness into the process to ensure that the outputs, while similar to the input data, are not just carbon copies but original works in their own right.

Through these technologies, Generative AI is not just imitating but innovating, bringing a touch of AI-driven creativity to tasks that were once thought to be exclusively human. Whether it's creating new fashion lines or dreaming up fantastical creatures for a video game, Generative AI is the artist with an algorithmic soul.

Ethical Considerations and Challenges of Generative AI

As Generative AI continues to paint its way across the digital canvas of our world, creating everything from art to synthetic data, it brings with it a palette of ethical considerations and challenges. This technology, while innovative and transformative, treads a fine line between creativity and controversy, raising questions about authenticity, privacy, and the very nature of art and authorship.

The Authenticity and Originality Debate

One of the most pressing ethical concerns surrounding Generative AI is the question of authenticity and originality. When an AI generates a piece of music or a work of art, who is the true creator? Is it the developer who designed the AI, the AI itself, or the data on which the AI was trained? This debate extends into copyright law, challenging our traditional notions of ownership and intellectual property. As Generative AI blurs the lines between human and machine creativity, society must grapple with redefining what it means to create and own a piece of art.

- **The Copycat Conundrum:** Generative AI's ability to produce works in the style of existing artists or to replicate the nuances of specific genres raises concerns about imitation versus inspiration. The potential for AI to flood the market with derivative works could undermine the value of original human creativity, making it harder for artists to sustain themselves through their art.

Privacy and Data Ethics

Another ethical challenge lies in the realm of data privacy and ethics. Generative AI's prowess, particularly in creating synthetic datasets, hinges on its access to vast amounts of data. While synthetic data can mitigate some privacy concerns by providing anonymized datasets for training other AI models, the process still involves the use of real data at some point. Ensuring that this data is sourced and utilized in a manner that respects individual privacy and consent is paramount.

- **The Synthetic Solution**: While synthetic data presents a promising solution to privacy concerns, it also raises questions about the accuracy and bias of the data generated. Ensuring that synthetic datasets do not perpetuate or exacerbate existing biases in AI models is a critical challenge that researchers and developers must address.

The Future of Work

Generative AI also prompts us to reconsider the future of work, particularly in creative industries. As AI becomes capable of performing tasks traditionally reserved for humans, from writing articles to designing buildings, the potential displacement of human workers becomes a significant concern. Balancing the benefits of AI-driven efficiency and innovation with the need to preserve human livelihoods and creativity is a delicate task.

- **Collaboration, Not Replacement**: The goal should be to leverage Generative AI as a tool that augments human creativity and productivity, rather than replacing it. Encouraging collaboration between humans and AI can lead to unprecedented levels of creativity and innovation, opening up new opportunities for artists, designers, and creators.

Navigating the Ethical Landscape

As we navigate the ethical landscape of Generative AI, it's clear that transparency, accountability, and thoughtful regulation will be key to harnessing its potential while mitigating its risks. Engaging in open dialogues between technologists, ethicists, artists, and policymakers will be crucial in developing frameworks that encourage innovation while protecting individual rights and promoting the equitable distribution of AI's benefits.

Generative AI, with its algorithmic soul, stands at the intersection of technology and creativity, offering a glimpse into a future where art and innovation flourish. Yet, going forward into the future, we must also navigate the ethical considerations and challenges it presents, ensuring that Generative AI serves to enhance human creativity and well-being, rather than diminish it.

DIVING DEEPER INTO AI AND GENERATIVE AI
DATA: THE FUEL OF AI

Welcome to the engine room of Artificial Intelligence and Generative AI. Here lies the most critical and potent resource in the AI arsenal: data. It's the fuel that powers the complex machinery of algorithms and models, and without it, the vibrant world of AI would grind to a halt. But not all fuel is created equal, and not all of it burns cleanly. In this chapter, we'll explore the multifaceted world of data, the ethical considerations surrounding its use, and why the quality of this data is vital to the integrity and utility of AI applications.

Understanding Data Types and Sources

In the intricate ballet of Artificial Intelligence, data is the stage upon which all algorithms perform. Just as a diverse repertoire enriches a performance, a variety of data types and sources enhances AI's potential. Let's draw back the curtain on the world of data types and their origins, examining how each plays its role in the grand performance of AI.

Data Types: The Cast of Characters

Data, the prima donna of the AI world, comes in two main types: structured and unstructured.

Structured Data: This is data that lives in predefined formats, typically rows and columns, like the disciplined lines of a spreadsheet or a database. Think of it as the classical ballet dancer of data. It's clean, precise, and easy to follow—every leap and pirouette can be predicted and quantified. Examples include customer information in a CRM system, sales figures in financial software, or sensor data from IoT devices.

Unstructured Data: Here's where the improvisational jazz musicians of the data world take the stage. Unstructured data is everything that doesn't fit neatly into a database. It's the social media posts, the emails, the images, videos, and the myriad of PDFs and Word documents. This data is rich in information but requires a complex choreography of processing to extract usable insights.

Sources: The sources of data are as varied as the venues where artists perform, each offering a different ambiance and audience.

First-Party Data: Collected directly from users, first-party data is like an intimate theater where the audience willingly participates in the show. This data is gathered from customer interactions, surveys, and subscription services, giving a clear and direct insight into consumer behavior.

Second-Party Data: This is like a co-production between troupes, where data is shared or purchased from a partner who has directly collected it. It's more like a collaborative festival, often specific and relevant, much like sharing mailing lists between trusted partners.

Third-Party Data: The large-scale concert halls of the data world, third-party data is aggregated from various sources by data providers who then sell it to companies. It's vast and varied but can sometimes lack the intimate nuances that make first and second-party data so valuable.

DATA COLLECTION: THE CHOREOGRAPHY

The art of collecting data is a choreography in itself. There are APIs pulling in torrents of social media data, web scraping tools that gather public data from the internet, sensors collecting real-time information from the environment, and transactional systems that record every purchase and interaction.

With such a multitude of sources, AI systems can be fed a rich diet that allows them to learn deeply about human behavior, societal trends, or operational efficiencies. But as with any performance, the quality of the output is directly related to the input. Garbage in, garbage out, as the adage goes—feed an AI poor quality data, and its insights will be equally poor.

In summary, understanding data types and sources is akin to appreciating the diverse performances of a festival. Each type and source offers its own unique insights and challenges, and mastering their use is key to the successful application of AI. Whether structured or unstructured, first-party or third-party, the data we collect is the fuel that powers the AI revolution, driving it forward into uncharted territories of innovation and discovery.

Data Ethics and Privacy

In the ever-expanding digital universe, data is the currency, and with great data comes great responsibility. Ethics and privacy are the guardians at the gate, ensuring that when we harness data to fuel AI, we do so with respect for the individuals behind the numbers and the societies they represent.

Ethical Considerations: The Moral Compass

Ethics in data is about navigating the gray. It's about asking not just what we can do with data, but what we should do. This involves consent, where individuals willingly share their information, knowing how it will be used. It's about transparency, ensuring that the data subjects are aware of the data collection process and its purpose. It's about fairness, ensuring that AI doesn't perpetuate biases or widen inequalities.

One must consider the balance between beneficial data use and individual rights. For example, while health data can be used to fuel medical breakthroughs, it's also deeply personal. Ethical AI seeks to use such data to benefit individuals and society while safeguarding personal dignity.

Privacy Laws: The Rulebook

Privacy laws are the rulebook for this game, and they vary widely across the globe, reflecting differing cultural norms and values.

General Data Protection Regulation (GDPR): In the EU, GDPR sets the stage, focusing on protecting citizens' personal data. It enforces the principles of data minimization, purpose limitation, and consent, among others.

California Consumer Privacy Act (CCPA): In the U.S., California has taken the lead with the CCPA, which grants consumers rights over their data, including the right to know, the right to delete, and the right to opt-out of the sale of personal information.

Personal Data Protection Act (PDPA): Asia also steps into the ring with regulations like Singapore's PDPA, which controls the process of personal data by organizations in an effort to strengthen the security and privacy of individuals' personal data.

Across all these laws, the common thread is the empowerment of individuals over their personal data, granting them a say in how their data is used and by whom.

Implementing Ethics and Privacy: The Application

The implementation of ethical practices and privacy laws in AI requires a blend of technology, policy, and vigilance. It's about embedding privacy into the design of AI systems (Privacy by Design), conducting Data Protection Impact Assessments (DPIAs), and continuously monitoring the use of AI to ensure it aligns with ethical standards and legal requirements.

For AI developers and data scientists, this means considering the impact of their creations on privacy from the get-go. For companies, it means establishing a culture of data protection and educating stakeholders about the importance of data ethics.

In summary, data ethics and privacy are not just legal requirements but moral imperatives that ensure the advancement of AI technologies aligns with the values of trust, respect, and fairness. Moving forward, these considerations will remain central to the conversation, ensuring that AI serves humanity without infringing upon the rights that make us human.

Importance of Quality Data

In the grand scheme of AI, the adage "quality over quantity" has never been more pertinent. Quality data is the linchpin of reliable, effective AI systems. It's like the difference between a gourmet meal and fast food; both can satisfy hunger, but the former offers a far more enriching experience.

The Crux of Quality Data

Quality data is accurate, complete, relevant, and timely. It reflects the real-world scenario it's meant to represent without distortion. High-quality data is to AI what clean air is to breathing; it's essential for the health and functionality of the system.

Consider the ramifications of low-quality data:

Inaccuracies: Just as a single typo can change the meaning of a sentence, inaccurate data can lead to flawed AI decisions. For instance, if an AI system training on clinical data is fed incorrect patient records, it could lead to misdiagnoses.

Biases: Data is not immune to human prejudices. Biases in data can lead to AI models that discriminate, unintentionally perpetuating stereotypes. Imagine a job application filtering AI trained on data reflecting historical hiring biases against certain demographics—it would continue the cycle of discrimination.

Incompleteness: Incomplete data can skew AI insights, leading to decisions made without considering the full picture. This is akin to solving a puzzle with missing pieces; the final image will be distorted.

Data Cleaning: The Art of Refinement

The process of refining raw data into quality data is known as data cleaning. It involves correcting inaccuracies, filling in missing values, smoothing out noise, and removing irrelevant information. This process is meticulous and can be as complex as the data itself.

Data cleaning is not just about scrubbing away the bad but also about enriching the data. It can involve techniques like:

Data Augmentation: Enhancing data by adding carefully constructed data points can help AI systems learn more robustly.

Normalization: Adjusting data scales to a common range can make learning more efficient and prevent models from misinterpreting the relative importance of different features.

The Ripple Effect of Quality Data

The impact of quality data ripples through every layer of AI. With a solid foundation of quality data, AI models can achieve:

Better Performance: Just as high-quality ingredients can improve a dish's flavor, quality data can enhance an AI model's accuracy and reliability.

Generalization: Quality data helps AI systems to generalize from the training environment to real-world applications. It's the difference between a sheltered existence and being world-wise.

Trustworthiness: When AI systems make decisions based on quality data, users can trust the outcomes. This trust is crucial for AI adoption in sensitive fields like healthcare and finance.

In essence, quality data is not just important—it's imperative for the creation of AI systems that are not only intelligent but also fair, unbiased, and reliable. As we continue to advance in the land of AI, the focus on cultivating and maintaining quality data must remain at the forefront, ensuring that the AI of tomorrow is built on the solid ground of today's best data practices.

COMPUTING POWER: THE MUSCLE BEHIND AI

The narrative of artificial intelligence is deeply intertwined with the evolution of computing power. This symbiotic relationship has propelled AI from the kingdom of science fiction into the fabric of our daily lives, powering everything from the virtual assistants in our smartphones to the algorithms that predict climate change. Let's delve deeper into how advancements in computing power have been pivotal in the development and application of AI.

The Evolution of Computing Power

The odyssey of computing power, from the behemoth mainframes of yesteryears to today's sleek, energy-efficient processors, mirrors the journey of AI from obscurity to ubiquity. Each technological leap has not only expanded the horizons of what's possible with AI but also democratized access to these powerful tools.

- **From Mainframes to Microprocessors**: The transition from bulky, inefficient mainframes to compact, powerful microprocessors represents a quantum leap in computing technology. This shift made computing power more accessible, laying the groundwork for the personal computer revolution and, subsequently, for the proliferation of AI technologies. Microprocessors brought the processing power necessary for complex computations closer to the masses, enabling the development and deployment of AI on a scale previously unimaginable.

- **The GPU Revolution**: The advent of Graphics Processing Units (GPUs) marked a significant milestone in the AI saga. Originally designed to render images for video games, GPUs found an unexpected application in AI for their ability to perform multiple calculations simultaneously. This parallel processing capability made GPUs particularly suited for the matrix and vector operations that are fundamental to machine learning and deep learning algorithms. By drastically reducing the time required for data processing and model training, GPUs have accelerated the pace of AI research and development.

- **The Rise of Specialized AI Chips**: As AI applications become more complex and demanding, the need for more specialized computing solutions has led to the development of AI-specific chips. These chips are engineered to optimize the efficiency of AI tasks, such as neural network processing and machine learning model inference. By integrating capabilities like tensor processing and neural network acceleration, specialized AI chips offer a significant boost in performance and energy efficiency. This specialization is making AI more scalable and sustainable, enabling more sophisticated applications across a broader range of devices and platforms.

Cloud Computing: Democratizing Access to AI

Cloud computing has emerged as a transformative force in the field of artificial intelligence, leveling the playing field and enabling a broader spectrum of innovators to contribute to the advancement of AI technologies. This democratization of access is reshaping the landscape of AI development, making it more inclusive, dynamic, and innovative.

Breaking Down Barriers

The advent of cloud computing has significantly lowered the entry barriers to AI development. Previously, the high costs associated with acquiring and maintaining the necessary hardware and infrastructure limited AI research and development to well-funded corporations and institutions. Cloud computing has changed this dynamic by offering AI processing power as a service.

- **Cost-Effective Solutions**: Startups, independent researchers, and educational institutions can now tap into the same level of computing resources as their larger counterparts, but without the hefty upfront investment. This pay-as-you-go model allows for the efficient allocation of resources, ensuring that even projects with limited budgets can explore AI innovations.

- **Access to Cutting-Edge Technology**: Cloud platforms continuously update their offerings with the latest hardware and software, providing users with access to state-of-the-art AI processing capabilities. This ensures that AI developers can always work with the most advanced tools available, fostering a culture of continuous improvement and innovation.

Scalability and Flexibility

One of the key advantages of cloud computing in the context of AI is its inherent scalability and flexibility. The ability to scale computing resources up or down on demand is crucial for AI projects, which often have variable computational requirements.

- **Dynamic Resource Allocation**: Whether it's the intensive computational power needed to train deep learning models or the more modest requirements for deploying AI-driven applications, cloud computing can dynamically adjust to meet these needs. This elasticity not only optimizes resource utilization but also ensures that projects can be scaled according to their success and demand.

- **Global Accessibility**: The cloud's global nature means that computing resources are available from anywhere, at any time. This accessibility supports a more flexible approach to AI development, where teams can work across different time zones and geographical locations, leveraging the cloud's infrastructure to collaborate effectively.

Collaboration and Innovation

Perhaps one of the most significant impacts of cloud computing on AI is its facilitation of collaboration and innovation. The cloud acts as a global platform where ideas, data, and tools can be shared freely, fostering a collaborative environment that accelerates the pace of AI advancements.

- **Shared Data and Tools**: Cloud platforms offer a wealth of shared resources, from open-source AI frameworks and libraries to vast datasets. This communal pool of resources encourages a collaborative approach to problem-solving, where developers can build upon each other's work, avoiding duplication of effort and accelerating the development process.

- **Rapid Prototyping and Deployment**: The cloud enables developers to quickly prototype new AI applications, test their ideas in real-world scenarios, and deploy successful projects at scale. This rapid iteration cycle is crucial for innovation, allowing developers to experiment freely and adapt their approaches based on feedback and results.

Cloud computing has fundamentally changed the game for AI development, offering a platform that supports the scalability, flexibility, and collaboration needed to drive forward the next generation of AI innovations. As cloud technologies continue to evolve, they will undoubtedly play an even more significant role in shaping the future of artificial intelligence, making it more accessible, powerful, and impactful than ever before.

Challenges and Future Directions in AI Computing Power

The journey of AI is one of remarkable progress and promise, yet it navigates a landscape filled with challenges that must be addressed to ensure its sustainable and ethical growth. The exponential increase in computing power has propelled AI to new heights, but this ascent brings with it concerns about energy consumption, environmental impact, and the limits of current technology.

Navigating the Energy Challenge

The computational demands of training sophisticated AI models have surged, leading to an increase in energy consumption that poses significant environmental challenges. As AI becomes more integrated into our daily lives, the urgency to find sustainable solutions grows.

- **Energy Efficiency**: The quest for energy efficiency in AI computing is multifaceted, involving the optimization of algorithms to reduce computational waste, the development of more energy-efficient hardware, and the adoption of renewable energy sources in data centers. Innovations such as spiking neural networks, which mimic the human brain's energy efficiency, offer promising avenues for reducing the power requirements of AI systems.
- **Sustainable Practices**: Beyond technological solutions, there's a movement towards adopting more sustainable practices in AI research and development. This includes the use of carbon offsetting for AI-related energy consumption and the prioritization of energy efficiency as a key factor in the design and deployment of AI systems. By embracing these practices, the AI community can mitigate its environmental impact while continuing to advance the field.

Quantum Computing: The Next Frontier

Quantum computing represents a paradigm shift in our approach to computational challenges, offering a glimpse into a future where the current limitations of AI could be transcended.

- **Beyond Classical Limits**: Quantum computers leverage the principles of quantum mechanics to process information in ways that classical computers cannot. This quantum advantage could dramatically accelerate tasks such as optimization, material simulation, and complex problem-solving, which are critical to advancing AI.
- **AI and Quantum Synergy**: The intersection of quantum computing and AI holds the potential for mutual acceleration. Quantum algorithms could enhance AI's ability to learn and make decisions, while AI could optimize quantum computing algorithms and hardware design. This synergy could lead to breakthroughs in fields ranging from drug discovery to climate modeling, where the computational challenges have long outpaced the capabilities of classical computing.

Looking Ahead: Ethical and Practical Considerations

As we stand on the brink of these technological advancements, it's crucial to navigate the ethical and practical considerations that accompany them.

- **Accessibility and Equity**: Ensuring that the benefits of advanced computing technologies like quantum computing are accessible to a broad range of researchers and institutions is vital for fostering an equitable AI landscape. This includes addressing the digital divide and supporting open research initiatives.

- **Security Implications**: The power of quantum computing brings with it security implications, particularly in the world of cryptography. Preparing for a post-quantum world, where traditional encryption methods may no longer be secure, is an essential challenge that researchers and policymakers are beginning to address.

The future of AI, powered by advancements in computing technology, is bright with potential. Yet, it's imperative to address the challenges of energy efficiency, environmental sustainability, and the ethical deployment of emerging technologies like quantum computing. By tackling these issues head-on, we can ensure that the growth of AI contributes positively to society, opening up new frontiers of knowledge and capability without compromising the health of our planet or the integrity of our digital world.

MACHINE LEARNING BASICS

Supervised vs. Unsupervised vs Semi- Supervised Learning

Venturing into the world of machine learning is akin to stepping into a classroom. There are two teaching styles you'll quickly become acquainted with: supervised and unsupervised learning. Both have their charm, quirks, and a unique way of leading algorithms through the school of data.

Supervised Learning: The Classroom with a Lesson Plan

Supervised learning is the straight-A student of machine learning. It's all about learning with clear direction and an answer key. In this setup, every piece of data comes with a label, like a sticky note explaining what it is. It's like teaching a dog to fetch; you throw the ball (input) and expect the dog to bring it back (the predicted output).

Imagine you're teaching your computer to differentiate between cats and dogs. You'd show it thousands of photos, each neatly labeled "cat" or "dog." The algorithm studies the features associated with each label, learning, for example, that pointy ears and a penchant for climbing curtains likely indicate a cat. Supervised learning algorithms can be real know-it-alls because they're trained on this labeled data until they can predict the label without seeing the sticky note.

Common supervised learning algorithms include linear regression for predicting continuous outcomes and logistic regression, support vector machines, or neural networks for classification tasks that spit out discrete labels.

Unsupervised Learning: The Freeform Art Class

Unsupervised learning, on the other hand, is like that cool art teacher who tells you to express yourself with clay without giving you a picture of what to sculpt. It deals with data that's as unlabeled as a hipster's homebrewed kombucha. The algorithm is left to its own devices to find structure in the data, like clustering together data points that seem to be BFFs based on their features.

A classic example is the cocktail party algorithm, where the AI listens to a jumble of noises and voices and learns to separate them into individual conversations. There are no "correct" answers here; unsupervised learning is all about discovery. It's great for market segmentation, where businesses can identify distinct customer groups without predefined categories, or for social network analysis, figuring out who hangs out with whom in the vast playground of social media.

The star players in unsupervised learning include k-means clustering, where the AI tries to find the cliques in the data, and principal component analysis, which is like reducing a gourmet meal to its essential flavors.

Hybrid Approach: Semi-supervised Learning

And then there's the middle child that sometimes gets overlooked: semi-supervised learning. It operates with a mix of labeled and unlabeled data. It's perfect for when you've got a lot of data but labeling it all would be as tedious as watching paint dry.

In Detail:

To truly master these concepts, consider the following nuances:

Data Preparation: For supervised learning, you need a meticulously labeled dataset. It's a bit like meal prepping for the week—you have to invest time upfront. For unsupervised learning, you can dive in with raw, unlabeled data. It's like foraging in the wilderness of information.

Outcome Predictions: In supervised learning, the outcome of the algorithm is typically known and defined, whether it's the price of a house or identifying spam emails. Unsupervised learning is more exploratory, searching for patterns or groupings without knowing in advance what it might find.

Real-World Applications: Supervised learning helps with targeted problems, like predicting stock prices or diagnosing diseases from symptoms. Unsupervised learning shines when you're not quite sure what you're looking for, like trying to understand customer behavior from website data without any preconceived notions.

By understanding these two distinct learning styles, you're better equipped to choose the right approach for your data dilemma. Supervised learning demands a well-prepped dataset and a clear goal, while unsupervised learning is your go-to when you're data-rich but knowledge-poor and ready to explore. Both approaches offer a pathway to extracting insights from data—just remember, the path you choose will shape the journey of your AI project.

Common Algorithms and Their Uses

In the theatrical production of Artificial Intelligence, machine learning algorithms are the cast members, each with a distinctive role that propels the plot forward. These algorithms are the silent heroes behind the AI systems we use daily. Here's a combined synopsis of some key players, complete with real-world applications to help illustrate their functions.

Linear Regression: The Predictor Extraordinaire

Linear regression is the straight shooter of the algorithm world. It's employed when we need a reliable projection of future trends based on historical data. Real estate agents use it to estimate property values by examining factors like square footage and neighborhood demographics. Economists may call upon it to forecast economic growth or unemployment rates. The algorithm's ability to draw a best-fit line through data points makes it indispensable for predicting continuous variables.

Logistic Regression: The Binary Oracle

Despite "regression" in its name, logistic regression is all about classification. Medical fields often use it to determine the likelihood of a patient having a particular condition, translating complex medical readings into a simple "yes" or "no" diagnosis. In finance, it might assess the probability of a credit card transaction being fraudulent. This algorithm deals in the currency of probabilities, providing binary outcomes that guide crucial decisions.

Decision Trees: The Decision Architects

Decision trees carve out paths of choices, branching out into increasingly specific segments. They're the flowchart wizards, mapping out the journey of decision-making. Financial institutions may deploy decision trees to navigate the maze of loan approval, sorting applicants into 'approved' or 'denied' based on their financial profiles. In customer service, decision trees can route customer inquiries to the appropriate department, streamlining the resolution process.

Random Forest: The Ensemble of Insight

Random Forest gathers an ensemble of decision trees to form a more accurate and robust predictive force. It's like a council of wise old trees in a fantasy novel, each providing its own insight to arrive at the best collective decision. In healthcare, Random Forest could analyze a myriad of patient data points to predict disease outbreaks with higher accuracy than any lone decision tree could achieve.

Support Vector Machines (SVM): The Discerning Dividers

SVMs are the bouncers of the data club, drawing lines that define who's in and who's out. Their knack for classification makes them ideal for image recognition tasks. Biologists might use SVMs to categorize species in wildlife photographs, while security systems employ them to distinguish between benign and threatening figures in surveillance footage.

K-Means Clustering: The Pattern Detectives

K-means clustering excels in uncovering hidden patterns within data. Retailers leverage this unsupervised algorithm to segment their customer base into clusters based on shopping habits, which can then inform targeted marketing strategies. In social media, k-means might analyze clusters of user activity to recommend new friends or content in line with a user's apparent preferences.

Neural Networks: The Mimickers of Human Brain

Neural networks are a bit like a band playing together; each neuron (musician) processes a small part of the task, and together they produce the final output (song). They're used in predictive typing, where, based on the sequence of the last few words you typed, the algorithm predicts what you'll type next.

Deep Learning: The Multilayered Thinkers

Deep Learning algorithms are the virtuosos of the machine learning world, handling complex tasks like language translation in real-time. They can process layers of data, identifying features that simpler algorithms might miss. Think of them as the architects who, instead of looking at individual bricks, see the entire shape and structure of the building.

For Neural Networks and Deep Learning, while we'll only give them a brief nod here, know that they're behind many of the sophisticated AI applications you interact with daily, from your social media feed to your virtual assistant's voice recognition capabilities. We'll dive into the depths of these algorithms in the next chapter, exploring how they're modeling complex patterns and driving the frontier of AI innovation.

DEEP LEARNING AND NEURAL NETWORKS
WHAT ARE NEURAL NETWORKS?

Neural networks are a foundational concept in the field of AI, particularly within the world of deep learning. They are inspired by the structure and function of the human brain, attempting to mimic the way biological neurons signal to one another.

The Analogy of Neurons and Neural Networks

To understand neural networks, imagine a busy office where each employee is a neuron. Each neuron (employee) specializes in a particular task. When a neuron receives data (a task), it processes the data (completes the task) and passes on the results (reports) to the next neuron (colleague) in line.

In biological terms, neurons are interconnected cells in the brain that are responsible for receiving sensory input from the external world, sending motor commands to our muscles, and transforming and relaying electrical signals at every step in between. Similarly, in an artificial neural network, individual units (artificial neurons) receive input, process the input, and generate output based on a predefined set of rules and learned experiences.

Components of Neural Networks

A typical neural network consists of:

Input Layer: This is where the network receives its input, similar to the senses in a human being. It's like the front desk of the office, receiving information from various sources.

Hidden Layers: These layers are where the processing happens. They can be thought of as the various departments within the office, each working on a specific aspect of the data. The complexity of the hidden layers can vary, leading to the concept of 'deep' networks with many layers.

Output Layer: The final layer provides the output, much like the finished product or service that leaves the office. For a classification task, this could be the category labels; for a regression task, this could be a continuous value.

How Neural Networks Learn

Neural networks learn similarly to how a new employee learns a job. They start with initial guidelines (randomly initialized weights), and as they are exposed to various situations (training data), they adjust their understanding (weights) to improve their performance.

Through a process called backpropagation, the network adjusts its weights. This is similar to an employee receiving feedback on their work and using it to do better next time. The 'learning rate' determines how quickly a neural network changes its weights. Too fast, and it might overlook important details; too slow, and it may take too long to learn.

In summary, neural networks are a powerful tool for modeling complex patterns in data. They can learn to perform a vast array of tasks, from recognizing faces to understanding natural language. They are not just lines of code; they are systems designed to learn from data, adapt to it, and make decisions or predictions—much like a brain, but with silicon neurons.

UNDERSTANDING DEEP LEARNING

Deep Learning is the virtuoso of the AI ensemble, capable of interpreting complex data symphonies with a finesse that's reshaping what machines can do.

The Significance of Deep Learning:

The key to deep learning's success is its ability to automate predictive analytics at scale. It's like having a digital detective with a magnifying glass sifting through data, finding patterns invisible to the naked eye. This detective is so adept that it's revolutionizing fields from healthcare, with its ability to spot disease markers in medical images, to customer service, where it powers responsive chatbots that seem to understand us better than we do ourselves.

Why Is Deep Learning 'Deep'?

The 'deep' in deep learning isn't just about depth of insight but also refers to the multiple processing layers through which data is transformed. These layers can be imagined as the layers in a complex cake, each adding a different flavor to the final outcome. Starting with simple patterns and moving to increasingly abstract concepts, deep learning models develop a nuanced understanding of the data they're fed.

The Achievements of Deep Learning:

Deep learning's achievements are no minor feats:

AlphaGo's Victory: More than a triumph over a human opponent, AlphaGo's innovative strategies have provided new insights into an ancient game.

Generative Models: They're not just imitating reality; they're creating new forms of it, from art to music, expanding the creative horizons beyond human limitations.

Medical Diagnostics: Deep learning models are assisting doctors by providing second opinions that are based on analyzing more medical data than any human could handle in a lifetime.

How Deep Learning Works:

Deep learning models work by passing input data through a series of layers, each refining and abstracting the information. It's similar to passing a concept through multiple experts, each adding their insight, resulting in a comprehensive understanding.

Training Deep Learning Models:

Training a deep learning model is a resource-intensive task that involves feeding large amounts of data into the model and allowing it to adjust its internal parameters. This process is akin to a long rehearsal where a musician practices until the tune is perfect. However, instead of hours, it might take days or weeks of computational time.

In conclusion, deep learning stands as a pinnacle of AI achievement, a blend of computational power and algorithmic design that's pushing boundaries across industries. Its ability to digest and interpret vast data sets makes it an invaluable tool for tackling some of the most challenging and impactful problems. As we continue to refine these models, their potential to innovate and enhance various aspects of life seems almost boundless.

Deep Learning Architectures: CNNs, RNNs, LSTMs, and GRUs

Convolutional Neural Networks (CNNs):

CNNs are often likened to an assembly line in a factory, where each station, or layer, specializes in recognizing different aspects of the visual data. The first layer might only pick out edges and basic textures, much like an employee on an assembly line who sorts parts by basic shapes. As data moves through subsequent layers, more complex features are identified—corners, contours, and eventually the high-level features that define the object's identity.

Deep Layers: In deeper layers, CNNs combine the simpler features from earlier layers to recognize complex patterns. For example, after identifying edges and textures, the network might combine these to recognize a pattern consistent with fur or whiskers.

Training: During training, CNNs use backpropagation to adjust the weights in the convolutional filters, honing their ability to highlight relevant features while suppressing noise.

Applications: Beyond image classification, CNNs are also used for tasks like object detection, where not only the objects need to be identified, but their locations within the image are also determined. For instance, in autonomous driving, a CNN helps detect pedestrians and traffic signs, ensuring safe navigation.

Recurrent Neural Networks (RNNs):

RNNs are designed to act like a sequence reader, where each word, note, or data point is a chapter in a story, and the plot depends on what's happened before. They're particularly well-suited for tasks like language modeling, where the meaning of a word can depend heavily on the words that come before it.

Feedback Loops: RNNs have feedback loops that allow information to persist. In practice, this means that during training, when an RNN processes a sentence, it keeps track of the context, which influences how it interprets the next word.

Vanishing Gradient Problem: Traditional RNNs can struggle with long sequences due to the vanishing gradient problem, where information from early in the sequence gets lost by the time the network processes the end.

Applications: RNNs shine in time-series prediction, like predicting the next day's stock prices based on historical data. They're also used for text generation, where each new word generated can depend on the entire previous sequence of words.

Long Short-Term Memory networks (LSTMs):

LSTMs can be seen as the solution to RNNs' forgetfulness. They have a more complex architecture that includes mechanisms to remember and forget information selectively.

Cell State: The cell state acts as a conveyor belt, running straight down the entire chain of the LSTM, with only minor linear interactions. It's very easy for information to flow along it unchanged.

Gates: The LSTM's gates can remove or add information to the cell state. The forget gate decides what information we're going to throw away from the cell state. The input gate decides which values we'll update, and the output gate decides what the next hidden state should be.

Applications: LSTMs have been successful in complex problem domains like machine translation, where maintaining context across long sentences is crucial, or in speech recognition, where understanding a phrase may depend on the entire conversation that preceded it.

Gated Recurrent Units (GRUs):

GRUs are a streamlined version of LSTMs, designed to be simpler and more computationally efficient, which can sometimes lead to similar performance.

Simplified Gates: GRUs combine the input and forget gates into a single "update gate" and merge the cell state and hidden state, resulting in a lighter model that's easier to train.

Reset Gate: The reset gate in GRUs allows the model to forget previous computations, which can be useful if the context of the problem changes significantly from one data point to the next.

Applications: GRUs are utilized in tasks where modeling sequential data is essential but the sequences are not extremely long, which can make them ideal for tasks like real-time language translation on mobile devices.

By understanding these architectures in depth, practitioners can select the most appropriate model for their specific task, whether they need the image-recognition prowess of CNNs, the sequence-processing power of RNNs, the long-term memory capabilities of LSTMs, or the efficiency and simplicity of GRUs. Each has a vital role to play in the evolving scenery of neural network design and application.

APPLICATIONS OF GENERATIVE AI

GENERATIVE AI IN ART AND CREATIVITY: UNVEILING NEW DIMENSIONS

The fusion of Generative AI with art and creativity heralds a digital renaissance, a period marked by an explosion of innovation and exploration that parallels the transformative eras of art history. This new wave of creativity is not just about the application of technology; it's about redefining the essence of artistic expression and collaboration.

The AI Artist's Toolkit: A Symphony of Algorithms

Generative AI introduces a toolkit that is as diverse as it is profound, offering artists an array of capabilities that transcend the traditional boundaries of medium and technique. This toolkit is not just a set of tools; it's a partner in the creative process, providing artists with the means to realize visions that were once confined to the imagination.

Visual Artistry Unleashed: In visual arts, Generative AI algorithms are capable of creating intricate patterns, textures, and compositions that mirror the complexity of human creativity. Artists can input thematic elements, color schemes, or stylistic preferences, and the AI can generate art that reflects these inputs with astonishing originality and depth.

The Music of Machines: In music, Generative AI is composing pieces that span genres and styles, from classical symphonies to contemporary electronic beats. By analyzing vast datasets of music, AI can generate compositions that resonate with human emotions, offering a new lens through which we can explore the universal language of music.

Expanding Creative Horizons: The Boundless Canvas

Generative AI empowers artists to transcend traditional creative limitations, enabling them to explore uncharted territories of expression. This boundless canvas is not just a metaphorical space; it's a tangible expansion of what's possible in art and creativity.

Materializing the Immaterial: Artists are using Generative AI to create works that blend the digital and physical worlds, crafting experiences that engage the senses in novel ways. From digital sculptures that can be experienced in virtual reality to AI-generated fashion that morphs in response to environmental stimuli, the potential for innovation is limitless.

Redefining Collaboration: The relationship between artist and AI is a dynamic form of collaboration that challenges our conventional understanding of creativity. This partnership is based on an iterative dialogue, where the output of the AI serves as both inspiration and foundation for further artistic exploration. It's a dance of ideas and algorithms, leading to creations that are both unexpected and profound.

Tools and Techniques in AI-Driven Art

In the vibrant gallery of AI-driven art, where the echoes of traditional creativity meet the whispers of the future, artists are now wielding tools that seem lifted from the pages of a science fiction novel.

Among these tools, Generative Adversarial Networks (GANs) stand out, accompanied by an ensemble of AI systems like Recurrent Neural Networks (RNNs), Long Short-Term Memory (LSTM) Networks, Variational Autoencoders (VAEs), and Convolutional Neural Networks (CNNs). This eclectic mix of technology blends the old with the startlingly new, creating a studio space where one might half-expect to find a coffee-making robot alongside the paintbrushes and chisels.

GANs, the rock stars of this AI art world, play a unique role, with one part of the network (the generator) producing art at a prolific rate and the other part (the discriminator) acting as the ever-critical judge. This dynamic duo battles it out to create artworks that range from eerily lifelike to the kind of pieces your cat might claim credit for on a lazy Sunday afternoon. But GANs aren't the only performers on this stage.

RNNs and LSTMs are the storytellers, weaving narratives and composing symphonies with a memory and finesse that keep the audience captivated.

They're the ones ensuring that the story doesn't lose its thread, making them perfect for generating coherent text and music that flows naturally, rather than meandering aimlessly.

VAEs, the shapeshifters of the group, excel in the art of transformation, mastering style transfer to morph ordinary images into masterpieces that blur the lines between reality and art. They navigate the identity crises of pixels, proving that even digital entities can undergo profound metamorphoses.

Meanwhile, CNNs serve as the keen-eyed observers of this artistic troupe, analyzing and understanding visual content with an acuity that rivals the most meticulous art critic. They're the backbone of image recognition and processing, ensuring that every detail, every nuance of the AI-generated art, is scrutinized and appreciated.

Together, these AI systems form a modern atelier, where the process of creating art is as fascinating as the artworks themselves. Artists engage with these technologies in a dance of creativity, employing iterative feedback loops to refine AI-generated outputs, adopting hybrid approaches that merge digital with physical, and delving into the algorithms themselves to customize the artistic output. This collaboration between human and machine is not just about producing art; it's about exploring new frontiers of creativity, where each brushstroke and pixel is a step into the unknown.

As we navigate this new era of AI-driven art, we're reminded that creativity is not a static trait, confined to the human mind, but a dynamic process that can be shared, augmented, and expanded in ways we're only beginning to understand. The fusion of AI systems like GANs, RNNs, LSTMs, VAEs, and CNNs with traditional artistic techniques is not just transforming the art we create; it's reshaping our very notions of what it means to be creative. In this world, the question isn't just "Can it make coffee?" but "Can it stir the soul?"

The Art of Collaboration: AI and Artist

The dance between artists and AI is a delicate one, involving more than just shouting commands into the void and hoping for a masterpiece in return. It's about understanding, iterating, and sometimes just trying to get along.

- **Iterative Feedback Loops**: Picture an artist and AI in a never-ending tango, where each step by the AI is adjusted and refined by the artist. It's a dance of "two steps forward, one step back," gradually moving towards a piece that might just be worthy of hanging on the fridge.
- **Hybrid Approaches**: Some artists like to mix it up, throwing AI-generated patterns into their physical paintings or sculptures. It's the art world's answer to fusion cuisine, blending digital and tangible in ways that can be surprisingly palatable.
- **Algorithmic Customization**: For the tech-savvy artist, tweaking AI algorithms is like seasoning a dish to taste. A pinch of code here, a dash of data there, and voilà, you've got something that's uniquely yours (and hopefully doesn't taste like computer chips).

Navigating the Ethical Palette

With great power comes great responsibility, and with great AI comes a whole palette of ethical considerations. From questioning the originality of AI-generated art to ensuring that your digital muse isn't just regurgitating stereotypes, artists are treading new ground.

- **Creative Autonomy vs. AI Influence**: It's a delicate balance between being inspired by AI and having your work overshadowed by it. Artists are finding ways to ensure that the final piece still reflects their vision, even if the AI suggests adding more cowbell.
- **Data Ethics**: Just as you wouldn't paint with stolen paint, using data ethically is paramount. Artists are becoming more mindful of the sources and implications of the data feeding their AI, ensuring their digital creations are both original and respectful.

Spotlight on Pioneers: Case Studies in AI-Driven Art

The collaboration between artists and AI has already produced remarkable projects that highlight the potential of this technology to revolutionize the art world.

- **Refik Anadol's Visionary Installations**: Anadol's work, particularly "Machine Hallucination," showcases how AI can analyze vast datasets to create immersive visual experiences. These installations invite viewers to reconsider the relationship between data and design, offering a glimpse into a future where art is both generated and experienced in entirely new ways.
- **Sougwen Chung's Collaborative Performances**: Chung's performances, where she draws alongside robotic arms powered by AI, exemplify the potential for human-machine collaboration in the creative process. This partnership not only produces unique artworks but also prompts reflection on the evolving role of the artist in the age of AI.
- **Daddy's Car: AI's Beatles-Inspired Tune:** Sony CSL's Flow Machines project created "Daddy's Car," a song composed by AI to mimic The Beatles' style. This innovative track demonstrates AI's ability to digest and creatively reproduce the essence of iconic music, resulting in a composition that feels both nostalgic and novel. "Daddy's Car" stands as a testament to the merging paths of AI technology and musical artistry, offering a glimpse into the future of music composition.

Ethical and Aesthetic Reflections

As Generative AI becomes more integrated into the art world, it raises important questions about ethics, originality, and the nature of creativity.

- **Navigating Authorship and Originality**: The use of AI in art creation challenges traditional notions of authorship. Determining the creator of an AI-generated piece—be it the artist who designed the algorithm, the AI itself, or a combination of both—complicates our understanding of originality and ownership in art.

- **Ethical Considerations**: The capacity of Generative AI to replicate and innovate upon existing art styles also brings ethical considerations to the forefront. Artists and developers must navigate these waters carefully, ensuring that AI-generated art respects the intellectual property of human creators and contributes positively to the cultural landscape.

- **The Evolution of Aesthetic Standards**: The introduction of AI-generated art is also influencing aesthetic values, expanding the definition of what is considered beautiful or meaningful in art. As audiences become more accustomed to the unique qualities of AI-generated works, our collective aesthetic sensibilities are likely to evolve, embracing a broader spectrum of creative expression.

Generative AI in art and creativity marks a significant milestone in the ongoing dialogue between technology and human expression. By blending algorithmic complexity with artistic vision, it opens up new avenues for creativity that were previously unimaginable. As we continue to explore this synergy, the art world stands on the brink of a new frontier, one where the digital muse not only inspires but also co-creates the art of tomorrow.

GENERATIVE AI IN BUSINESS AND MARKETING

In the bustling marketplace of the digital age, where businesses vie for attention like street performers on a crowded boulevard, Generative AI has emerged as the master illusionist, transforming the mundane into the magical. This new era of commerce is characterized by an unprecedented level of personalization and innovation, where every customer interaction can be as unique as a snowflake in a winter storm. Let's explore how Generative AI is redefining business and marketing, one algorithm at a time.

Personalization at Scale with Generative AI

The concept of personalization in business and marketing isn't new, but the scale and depth at which it can now be achieved with Generative AI are nothing short of revolutionary. This technology is enabling a level of individualized engagement that was previously unimaginable, transforming every digital interaction into a bespoke experience tailored to the individual's unique preferences and behaviors.

The Magic Behind the Curtain: Data as the New Gold

At the core of this transformative approach is an ocean of data, from browsing histories and purchase records to social media interactions and beyond. Generative AI dives into this vast digital expanse, surfacing with nuggets of insight that inform highly personalized marketing strategies. It's akin to having a digital alchemist who can turn raw data into personalized marketing gold.

- **Predictive Personalization**: Beyond reacting to past behaviors, Generative AI is predictive, forecasting future needs and desires based on complex patterns. This prescience allows businesses to not just meet but anticipate customer needs, offering solutions before the customer even recognizes the need themselves.
- **Dynamic Content Creation**: Imagine receiving an email that feels like it was written just for you, visiting a website that seems to morph to match your mood, or seeing a social media ad that speaks directly to your aspirations. Generative AI makes this possible by dynamically generating content that resonates on a personal level, making every digital interaction feel like a conversation with a friend who knows you well.

Beyond the Screen: Personalization in the Physical World

The impact of Generative AI-driven personalization extends beyond digital spaces, influencing how businesses interact with customers in the physical world.

- **Smart Retail Environments**: In the near future, we may see brick-and-mortar stores equipped with AI that personalizes the shopping experience in real-time. Imagine digital displays that change to show products you're likely to love or dressing rooms that suggest outfits based on your style preferences. Generative AI could turn shopping into a highly personalized adventure, where the store itself seems to understand and cater to your tastes.

- **Customized Products and Services**: Generative AI is also paving the way for the mass customization of products and services. From personalized skincare regimens formulated based on your genetic makeup to fitness plans tailored to your body's unique needs, AI's ability to analyze individual data points allows for customization at a scale previously deemed logistically impossible.

The Future of Personalization

As Generative AI continues to evolve, the frontier of personalization will expand even further. We're entering an era where businesses can create deeply personalized experiences that foster a genuine connection with their customers, transcending the transactional nature of commerce. This level of personalization not only enhances customer satisfaction and loyalty but also sets a new standard for what consumers expect from brands.

In this grand bazaar of the digital age, Generative AI stands as the master craftsman of personalization, weaving together the threads of data into a tapestry of individualized experiences. As businesses harness this technology, they're not just marketing products; they're curating experiences that resonate on a personal level, building lasting relationships in a world where digital and physical increasingly intertwine.

Product Development and Innovation with Generative AI

In the ever-evolving landscape of product development, where innovation is the currency of success, Generative AI is emerging as a pivotal force. This technology is not merely augmenting the creative process; it's redefining it, offering a glimpse into the future of consumer products and services. Let's delve deeper into how Generative AI is revolutionizing product development and innovation.

The Crystal Ball of Consumer Desires

Generative AI acts as a crystal ball, illuminating the path forward for product development by simulating consumer responses and predicting market trends. This foresight enables businesses to not just react to the market but to anticipate and shape it.

- **Predictive Design**: Imagine the ability to test hundreds of product designs in virtual environments, gauging consumer reactions to each before a single prototype is physically produced. Generative AI makes this possible, analyzing patterns in consumer data to predict which features, aesthetics, or functionalities will resonate most strongly with the market.

- **Customization at Scale**: In industries ranging from fashion to consumer electronics, the demand for personalized products is growing. Generative AI facilitates this trend by enabling the mass customization of products. For instance, AI algorithms can design custom apparel based on individual fashion preferences or create personalized user interfaces for smartphones that adapt to the user's habits and needs.

Designing the Future: A New Era of Innovation

Generative AI is not just predicting the future; it's helping to create it. By providing insights that drive innovation, AI is ensuring that new products not only meet but exceed consumer expectations.

- **Fashion Forward**: In the fashion industry, Generative AI is being used to predict upcoming trends, allowing designers to stay ahead of the curve. More than that, AI is being used to create innovative fabrics and materials, such as clothes that adapt to weather conditions, enhancing both style and functionality.
- **Tech That Understands You**: In the realm of technology, products are becoming increasingly intuitive, thanks to Generative AI. From smart homes that adjust to your living patterns to apps that predict your needs throughout the day, AI is at the forefront of developing technology that seamlessly integrates into our lives.
- **Sustainable Solutions**: Beyond consumer convenience, Generative AI is playing a crucial role in driving sustainability in product development. By simulating the environmental impact of products and their lifecycle, AI helps companies innovate in ways that reduce waste and conserve resources, leading to more sustainable consumer products.

The Future of Product Development with Generative AI

As we stand on the brink of this new era of innovation, it's clear that Generative AI will continue to play a critical role in shaping the future of product development. Its ability to analyze vast amounts of data, predict consumer desires, and simulate the real-world impact of products makes it an invaluable tool for businesses looking to innovate responsibly and effectively.

The journey of product development, powered by Generative AI, is one of exploration and discovery. It's about creating products that not only meet the current needs of consumers but also anticipate the needs of tomorrow. In this dynamic interplay between technology and creativity, the possibilities are limitless. As businesses harness the power of Generative AI, they're not just designing products; they're crafting the future, one innovation at a time.

Marketing with Generative AI

The integration of Generative AI into marketing strategies has not only opened new avenues for creativity and personalization but also set new benchmarks for what can be achieved when technology meets commerce. Let's delve deeper into the real-world applications that highlight the transformative power of Generative AI in marketing.

The Tailored Campaign: Revolutionizing Engagement

A global retailer's innovative use of Generative AI to craft personalized marketing videos for each customer showcases the technology's potential to revolutionize customer engagement. By analyzing customer data, the AI was able to generate content that resonated on a personal level, leading to a significant uptick in engagement.

- **Behind the Scenes**: The AI system analyzed purchase history, browsing behavior, and customer feedback to create a unique narrative for each video. This level of customization ensured that every piece of content was highly relevant and engaging to the individual viewer, making them feel valued and understood.

- **Impact and Outcome**: The campaign not only led to an increase in sales but also enhanced brand loyalty. Customers appreciated the personalized approach, which stood out in a sea of generic marketing content. The success of this campaign underscores the potential of Generative AI to create marketing that is not just seen but felt.

The Predictive Prototype: Anticipating Consumer Needs

The case of a leading tech company employing Generative AI to simulate consumer reactions to a new product feature before its launch illustrates the predictive power of AI. This preemptive approach allowed the company to refine and perfect the feature, ensuring it met consumer expectations right out of the gate.

- **Strategic Innovation**: By creating a virtual testing ground, the company was able to gather insights into how real users would interact with the new feature, identifying potential issues and opportunities for improvement that would have been difficult to predict without AI.

- **Success Story**: The feature's launch became one of the most successful in the company's history, attributed largely to the precision with which it was developed and introduced to the market. This case study highlights how Generative AI can transform the product development process, turning guesswork into a precise science.

The Dynamic Website: Personalizing the Digital Experience

An online travel agency's use of Generative AI to dynamically personalize website content for each visitor demonstrates the technology's ability to enhance the digital customer experience. By tailoring the site to individual preferences and browsing history, the agency was able to significantly increase bookings.

- **Personalization in Action**: The AI system continuously analyzed visitor data to adjust the content, offers, and recommendations displayed on the website in real-time. This ensured that every user was presented with options that matched their interests, making the booking process smoother and more intuitive.
- **Driving Results**: The personalized approach led to a marked improvement in user engagement and conversion rates. Customers reported higher satisfaction with the booking experience, as the content felt curated specifically for them. This case study exemplifies the power of Generative AI to create a digital environment that adapts to and anticipates the needs of its users.

These case studies in marketing underscore the versatility and impact of Generative AI across different sectors and applications. By enabling personalized experiences, predictive product development, and dynamic digital environments, Generative AI is not just transforming marketing strategies—it's redefining the relationship between businesses and their customers. Looking to the future, the integration of AI into marketing and business practices promises to further blur the lines between technology and human intuition, creating a marketplace that is increasingly personalized, predictive, and dynamic.

GENERATIVE AI IN SCIENTIFIC RESEARCH AND INNOVATIONS

In scientific research and innovation, where every discovery is a step into the unknown, Generative AI has emerged as a powerful ally, propelling fields forward at an unprecedented pace. From the meticulous process of drug discovery to the vast universe of data analysis and simulation, AI is not just a tool but a transformative force. Let's explore how Generative AI is reshaping the world of scientific inquiry and breakthroughs.

Accelerating Drug Discovery with Generative AI

The path to bringing a new drug to market is notoriously complex and fraught with challenges, often described as a journey of a thousand miles that begins with a single step. Generative AI is transforming this trip, equipping scientists with a jetpack to navigate the vast landscape of chemical compounds with unprecedented speed and precision.

Revolutionizing the Discovery Process

Generative AI is not just another tool in the pharmaceutical toolkit; it's a paradigm shift in how drugs are discovered and developed. Traditional methods of drug discovery involve a painstaking process of trial and error, testing thousands of compounds in the hope of finding a few that show potential. Generative AI turns this process on its head, using algorithms to quickly sift through and analyze data on millions of compounds, identifying those with the most promise for development into effective treatments.

- **A New Frontier in Virtual Screening**: The power of Generative AI lies in its ability to predict the interactions between chemical compounds and biological targets with astonishing accuracy. This virtual screening process is akin to having a crystal ball that reveals which compounds are likely to bind to specific receptors or enzymes, inhibiting or activating them in ways that could treat disease. By pinpointing these promising candidates early on, researchers can focus their efforts more effectively, saving time and resources.

- **The Art of Molecule Optimization**: Once potential drug candidates are identified, the next challenge is to refine their structures to maximize efficacy and minimize side effects. Generative AI excels here as well, employing sophisticated algorithms to simulate millions of molecular variations. This process allows scientists to explore a vast space of chemical structures, identifying modifications that enhance the drug's performance and safety profile. It's like having an expert chemist who can instantly generate and evaluate countless new drug formulations, guiding the development of molecules that are not only potent but also well-tolerated by the body.

The Impact on Drug Development

The implications of Generative AI for drug discovery and development are profound. By dramatically accelerating the identification and optimization of new drug candidates, AI is helping to bring life-saving treatments to market faster than ever before. Diseases that were once considered untreatable are now within the range of possibility, as AI uncovers new pathways for therapeutic intervention and novel compounds that can be developed into effective drugs.

- **Speeding Up the Race Against Disease**: In the fight against rapidly evolving diseases, such as cancer and infectious diseases, time is of the essence. Generative AI is a game-changer, enabling researchers to keep pace with the changing panorama of disease by quickly identifying and developing new drugs.
- **Democratizing Drug Discovery**: The efficiency and cost-effectiveness of Generative AI also have the potential to democratize drug discovery, making it possible for smaller labs and organizations to participate in the search for new treatments. This could lead to a more diverse and innovative drug development ecosystem, with more players contributing to the global effort to combat disease.

Generative AI is redefining the boundaries of what's possible in drug discovery, turning the painstaking marathon of pharmaceutical development into a faster, more efficient sprint. As this technology continues to evolve, it promises to unlock new frontiers in medicine, bringing hope to patients around the world and opening up new avenues for treating complex diseases.

Data Analysis and Simulation

In the modern era of scientific research, the deluge of data generated across disciplines from biology to climate science represents both an unprecedented opportunity and a formidable challenge. The sheer volume and complexity of this data have stretched traditional analytical methods to their limits, often slowing the pace of discovery. Generative AI emerges as a beacon of innovation in this landscape, wielding the power to transform data analysis and simulation, thereby accelerating the journey from hypothesis to insight.

Deep Insights from Big Data

Generative AI stands at the forefront of the battle against the data deluge, armed with algorithms capable of sifting through and making sense of vast datasets. This capability is not just about handling the volume of data but about discerning the subtle patterns and correlations that lie hidden within it.

- **Unlocking Genomic Mysteries**: In genomics, for example, Generative AI can analyze sequences from thousands of organisms, identifying genetic markers linked to diseases that were previously undetectable. This not only accelerates the pace of genetic research but also opens new avenues for personalized medicine.
- **Stargazing with AI**: In astrophysics, where the data from telescopes and space missions can be overwhelming, Generative AI helps in identifying celestial objects and phenomena, parsing the signals from the noise in the search for exoplanets and understanding the cosmic web of dark matter.

These deep insights derived from big data are as difficult as finding needles in cosmic haystacks, where Generative AI not only finds the needles but also deciphers the story they tell.

Simulating the Unseen

Beyond data analysis, Generative AI's ability to simulate complex systems and scenarios offers a powerful tool for scientific exploration. This aspect of AI serves as a virtual laboratory, where ideas can be tested, and discoveries made without the constraints of the physical world.

- **Virtual Drug Trials**: In pharmaceuticals, Generative AI can simulate the interaction between drugs and human biology, predicting the efficacy and side effects of new compounds. This virtual approach to drug trials can significantly reduce the need for costly and time-consuming physical trials, speeding up the development of new treatments.
- **Climate Change Models**: In environmental science, Generative AI is used to simulate climate change scenarios, helping scientists understand potential future impacts and explore mitigation strategies. These simulations can model complex interactions between atmospheric conditions, ocean currents, and ice melt patterns, providing valuable insights into the dynamics of climate change.

Bridging Realities

Generative AI's role in data analysis and simulation is akin to having a multidimensional map of the unknown, where each insight and simulated outcome adds a layer of understanding to our knowledge of the world. By bridging the gap between the vastness of data and the limitations of human analysis, Generative AI is not just an analytical tool but a gateway to new realms of discovery.

- **Exploring What Ifs**: The power of simulation extends to exploring "what if" scenarios across scientific disciplines, from testing hypotheses in evolutionary biology to modeling the spread of pandemics. This ability to explore alternate realities and predict their outcomes is invaluable in preparing for future challenges and seizing emerging opportunities.

As Generative AI continues to evolve, its impact on data analysis and simulation is poised to grow, offering scientists and researchers a powerful ally in their quest to unravel the mysteries of the universe. The fusion of AI with scientific inquiry marks a new era of discovery, where the only limit is the imagination of those who dare to ask, "What if?"

Case Studies in Research: AI's Landmark Contributions

The transformative impact of Generative AI on scientific research is not just a promise for the future—it's a reality that's unfolding now. Across various fields, AI-driven methodologies are leading to breakthroughs that were once beyond reach. Two areas where Generative AI has made particularly notable contributions are protein structure prediction and climate modeling, showcasing the technology's potential to address some of the most pressing challenges of our time.

Protein Structure Prediction: Unraveling the Building Blocks of Life

One of the most groundbreaking applications of Generative AI has been into protein structure prediction, exemplified by the success of DeepMind's AlphaFold. This achievement represents a quantum leap in our ability to understand the building blocks of life.

- **The AlphaFold Breakthrough**: AlphaFold's ability to predict the 3D structures of proteins with unprecedented accuracy has been hailed as a solution to a 50-year-old grand challenge in biology. By accurately modeling how protein chains fold into three-dimensional shapes, AlphaFold provides insights into the machinery of life itself, offering clues to how proteins determine everything from cellular function to the cause of diseases.

- **Implications for Medicine and Biology**: The implications of this breakthrough are vast. With accurate models of protein structures, researchers can more effectively understand disease mechanisms, accelerate drug discovery, and even engineer novel proteins with beneficial properties. This leap forward opens the door to new treatments and therapies, potentially revolutionizing medical science and biotechnology.

Climate Modeling: Navigating the Future of Our Planet

In the critical fight against climate change, Generative AI is emerging as a key player in developing sophisticated models that can predict future climate conditions with greater precision.

- **Enhancing Climate Models**: Generative AI is being used to refine climate models, incorporating vast amounts of environmental data to simulate the complex interactions within Earth's climate system. These enhanced models can account for variables such as atmospheric chemistry, ocean currents, and ice melt dynamics, providing a more comprehensive picture of potential future climates.
- **Informing Policy and Action**: The advanced predictive capabilities of AI-driven climate models are invaluable for policymakers and environmental scientists. By offering more accurate forecasts of temperature changes, sea-level rise, and extreme weather events, these models inform global climate policy, helping to shape strategies for mitigation and adaptation. They serve as a crucial tool in our collective efforts to understand and combat the impacts of climate change, guiding decisions that will affect the future of our planet.

The Road Ahead: Challenges and Opportunities

While the contributions of Generative AI to protein structure prediction and climate modeling are significant, they also highlight the broader potential of AI in scientific research. These case studies exemplify how AI can unravel complex scientific mysteries, offering new pathways to discovery and innovation.

- **Cross-disciplinary Applications**: The success of AI in these areas paves the way for its application across other scientific disciplines, from materials science to energy research. As AI technologies continue to evolve, their potential to drive further breakthroughs grows, promising to unlock new frontiers in our quest for knowledge.
- **Collaboration Between AI and Scientists**: The future of scientific research lies in the synergy between human expertise and AI's analytical power. This collaboration will be key to tackling the

multifaceted challenges that lie ahead, from curing diseases to safeguarding our environment.

Generative AI's landmark contributions to protein structure prediction and climate modeling are just the beginning. As we continue to harness this technology, its role in propelling scientific research and innovation forward is set to expand, marking a new era of discovery where the possibilities are as limitless as our collective imagination.

TEXT GENERATION WITH AI

In the grand narrative of text generation AI, we've seen a cast of characters ranging from the early rule-based systems, which operated with the rigidity of a grammar school teacher armed with nothing but a red pen, to the Generative Pre-trained Transformer models, especially the prodigious GPT-3 and the later versions, which crafts prose with the finesse of a seasoned novelist.

Let's take a moment to appreciate the ride. It began with the simplicity of rule-based systems—those early attempts at mimicking human conversation that now seem quaint, like the telegraphs of the digital communication era. These systems were followed by the statistical models, the n-grams, which could predict text in a way that felt slightly more human, though they still couldn't quite capture the poetry of language.

Then came the age of neural networks, where models like RNNs and LSTMs began to grasp the flowing melodies of human speech, learning the rhythms and cadences that make our language dance. They brought us closer to an AI that could not just parrot back what it had heard but engage in a duet with its human counterparts.

Now, we find ourselves in the era of GPT, a model that doesn't just understand the rules of language—it plays with them. With a dash of creativity here and a sprinkle of context there, it writes with a nuance that's deliciously close to human. It's an AI that could pen an article, compose a sonnet, or conjure up a story from a mere prompt, leaving readers to wonder, "Was this really written by a machine?"

In this chapter, we'll explore how GPT models are changing the way we interact with text, from the way we write to the way we read. We'll peel back the curtain on these linguistic magicians to understand how they cast their spells. And, with just the right touch of humor to keep things lively, we'll see how GPT can be as playful with words as it is profound.

After all, in the world of Generative AI, the pen may be mightier than the sword, but the algorithm is mightier than the pen.

GPT: The Pinnacle of Text Generative AI

In the ever-evolving saga of artificial intelligence, the chapter on GPT-3 unfolds as a pivotal climax. This is the story of how a machine learned not just to understand but to weave words with the deftness of a master wordsmith. GPT-3, the latest in the lineage of Generative Pre-trained Transformer models, stands as a giant upon whose shoulders the future of AI-generated text will firmly stand.

GPT-3 is like the wizard of the AI, conjuring up paragraphs from the ether with an almost human touch. It's the AI we've long envisioned—one that doesn't just regurgitate information but shapes it into narratives, arguments, and dialogues that feel startlingly human. It's not just the complexity of the model or the vastness of its training data that makes GPT-3 remarkable—it's the subtlety with which it understands and generates language.

On the ride through the capabilities of GPT-3, we'll see it not just as a culmination of progress but as a beacon of possibility. From the mechanics of its inner workings to the poetry it can produce, GPT-3 represents the synergy of technology and human creativity. It's a testament to how far we've come and a hint at the wondrous places we're yet to go.

Technical Breakdown

Diving into the technical essence of GPT-3 is akin to peering into the inner workings of a grand clock, where every gear's turn is pivotal to the overall function. GPT-3, or Generative Pretrained Transformer 3, is a behemoth in the world of artificial intelligence, distinguished by its sheer scale and the intricacy of its design.

Architectural Ingenuity

At its core, GPT-3 is built upon the transformer architecture, a model that has revolutionized natural language processing. The transformer utilizes what is known as self-attention, a mechanism that allows the model to weigh the importance of each word in a sentence relative to all other words. This is essential for understanding context and generating coherent and relevant text.

Scale and Pre-training

With an unprecedented 175 billion parameters—variables that the model uses to make predictions—GPT-3 is trained on a diverse dataset sourced from books, websites, and other texts. This pre-training phase equips GPT-3 with a broad understanding of language, context, and world knowledge before it is fine-tuned for specific tasks.

Fine-Tuning to Precision

After pre-training, GPT-3 can be fine-tuned, where it undergoes additional training on a smaller, task-specific dataset. This process sharpens its abilities, allowing for more accurate responses in specific contexts, whether that be legal discourse, poetic composition, or technical writing.

Decoding Language: From Tokens to Tales

GPT-3 processes text as a series of tokens—units that can be words or parts of words. It predicts the next token by considering the tokens that come before it, using its parameters to generate probabilities. The result is a model that can continue a given text prompt in a way that is surprisingly human-like in its complexity and nuance.

Handling Context with Attention

The attention mechanism in GPT-3 doesn't treat all input tokens equally. Instead, it assigns different levels of importance to different tokens, allowing the model to focus on the most relevant parts of the input when making predictions. It's this attention to detail that enables GPT-3 to handle nuanced instructions and generate text that flows logically and engagingly.

Challenges and Limitations

Despite its sophistication, GPT-3 has limitations. Its text can sometimes veer off-topic or become repetitive over longer passages. Additionally, it may inadvertently amplify biases present in its training data. Addressing these challenges is an ongoing effort in the field of AI.

In essence, GPT-3 is a marvel not just of what we've taught machines to do, but of how they've learned to teach themselves. Its technical prowess opens up new vistas in text generation, offering a glimpse into a future where AI and human creativity continue to co-evolve, unlocking potential we're only beginning to grasp.

GPT-3.5: Conversational Brilliance Beyond GPT-3

A Notable Leap

The transition from GPT-3 to GPT-3.5 is comparable to upgrading from a reliable bicycle to a sleek sports car. GPT-3 was groundbreaking, but GPT-3.5 takes conversational AI to a whole new level.

Enhanced Conversational Depth

GPT-3.5 engages in conversations with a depth that GPT-3 could only dream of. It comprehends context over longer interactions, making it ideal for tasks like drafting emails, brainstorming ideas, or even providing detailed explanations. The conversations with GPT-3.5 feel less like text exchanges and more like meaningful dialogues.

Imagine you're discussing a complex topic with GPT-3.5. Unlike its predecessor, it doesn't lose track of the conversation's context. It remembers what you said earlier, allowing for more coherent and relevant responses. This makes it a superb tool for professionals, educators, and anyone looking for in-depth conversations with AI.

Fewer Prompts, More Context

One of the notable differences in GPT-3.5 is its ability to sustain conversations with fewer explicit prompts(we will discuss prompts and how to create them in a dedicated chapter later in the book). GPT-3 often required specific instructions at each turn to maintain context. In contrast, GPT-3.5 can keep the conversation going over several exchanges without the need for constant reminders.

This enhanced contextual understanding means you can have smoother, more natural interactions with the AI. It's as if you're conversing with an AI that truly comprehends what you're saying, reducing the need for repetitive instructions.

Reduced Repetition

In the world of GPT-3.5, repetitive responses are a thing of the past. Remember those moments when GPT-3 seemed to recycle the same answer, regardless of how you phrased a question? GPT-3.5 addresses this limitation effectively.

When you engage in a conversation with GPT-3.5, you're more likely to receive diverse and contextually relevant responses. This reduction in redundancy enhances the quality of interactions, ensuring that conversations remain engaging and productive.

Improved Handling of Complex Queries

GPT-3.5 excels when faced with complex questions or tasks. It can handle multi-step instructions, providing step-by-step solutions or engaging in intricate discussions. This level of versatility makes it a valuable tool for a wide range of applications.

Let's say you're a programmer seeking help with a coding challenge. GPT-3.5 can not only understand your queries but also guide you through the problem-solving process, offering code snippets and explanations along the way. Similarly, if you're a writer looking for creative input, GPT-3.5 can assist with brainstorming ideas, plot development, and even character creation.

The Bridge to GPT-4

As GPT-3.5 elevates the conversational AI scenery, it also serves as a bridge to the future, where GPT-4 awaits. The evolution from GPT-3 to GPT-3.5 offers a glimpse of the capabilities yet to come.

Enhanced Training

GPT-4's training promises to be even more comprehensive. It will build upon the foundation laid by GPT-3.5, incorporating a broader spectrum of knowledge and language nuances. This will result in AI models that are not just more knowledgeable but also more culturally aware.

Imagine GPT-4 as a scholar who has read an entire library of books, encompassing various genres, languages, and cultural contexts. When you ask it about literature, it won't just provide standard answers; it will offer insights and recommendations tailored to your unique preferences and interests.

Deeper Contextual Understanding

While GPT-3.5 excels in understanding context, GPT-4 is expected to take this further. It will likely possess an even more intuitive grasp of conversational subtleties, making interactions feel even closer to human-level understanding.

Imagine having a conversation with GPT-4 that not only recognizes sarcasm but responds with witty humor of its own. It's the evolution of AI from a helpful assistant to a genuine conversational partner.

Ethical Advancements

Ethical considerations will continue to evolve with GPT-4. Stricter content guidelines and enhanced bias detection mechanisms will be crucial steps towards responsible AI usage.

Imagine an AI that not only provides information but also actively discourages harmful or biased content. GPT-4 will aim to promote fairness, inclusivity, and accuracy in all interactions.

Enhanced Web Browsing Capabilities

Real-Time Information Retrieval: ChatGPT-4's browsing feature heralds a new wave of information accessibility. The AI can now pull in real-time data from the internet, allowing it to reference current events, access up-to-date scientific research, and even shop online, all while maintaining a text-based conversation.

Summarization and Synthesis: The ability to summarize web content empowers ChatGPT-4 to act as a powerful research assistant. It can condense lengthy articles into concise summaries, extract key points from complex documents, and synthesize information from multiple web sources to provide comprehensive answers.

Advanced Analytical Abilities

Data Processing: ChatGPT-4 is not just about words; it's also about numbers and patterns. With advanced data analysis features, it can process large datasets, identify trends, and even make predictions based on historical data. This makes it an invaluable tool for businesses, researchers, and anyone in need of data-driven insights.

Sophisticated Reasoning: Beyond raw data, ChatGPT-4 can engage in sophisticated reasoning. It can evaluate arguments, propose hypotheses, and engage in problem-solving activities that require logical and analytical thought processes.

DALL-E Integration

Bridging Text and Visuals: The integration with DALL-E, an AI system capable of generating images from textual descriptions, opens up new creative possibilities. ChatGPT-4 can describe a scene, and DALL-E can create a corresponding image, facilitating a harmonious interplay between text and visuals.

Plugin System

Dynamic Extensions: The plugin system in ChatGPT-4 acts as a gateway to extended functionalities, transforming the AI from a standalone conversational agent to a central hub for various applications. This system equips ChatGPT-4 with the ability to perform a myriad of tasks that were previously out of reach for a language model.

Collaborative Ecosystem: The plugin architecture encourages a collaborative ecosystem where developers can contribute new functionalities. This collaborative spirit not only expands the capabilities of ChatGPT-4 but also fosters innovation, as the community can build upon each other's work to create a rich tapestry of tools.

Content Creation with Chat GPT: Unleashing Creativity

In the world of content creation, GPT-3.5 and GPT-4 emerge as revolutionary tools that empower writers, marketers, and creators to push the boundaries of their imagination. These AI models are not just digital scribes; they are creative collaborators, ready to assist in generating content across various domains.

Writing Assistance:

Unleashing Creativity:

Blog Posts and Articles: Chat GBT can be your research assistants, scouring the internet for the latest data and insights to include in your articles. They not only generate content but also ensure it aligns with your chosen niche and style.

Example: You're working on a blog post about travel destinations in Europe, focusing on Italy. You want to create an engaging charming streets and rich history of Italy.

You provide Chat GBT with this prompt: "Please help me craft an opening paragraph for my blog post about exploring the *Marketing Copy"*

These AI models are like having a marketing guru on your team. They understand the nuances of persuasive language and can generate ad copy that grabs attention, drives engagement, and ultimately boosts conversion rates.

Creative Writing: For authors and screenwriters, collaborating with Chat GBT is essentially having an endless brainstorming session. They can help you brainstorm plot twists, character arcs, and even generate dialogues that keep readers or viewers hooked.

As a fiction writer, you're looking to develop a unique antagonist character for your fantasy novel set in a magical realm. You provide ChatGPT with the prompt: "Create a character profile for the main antagonist of my fantasy novel. Describe their appearance, personality, motivations, and any distinctive magical abilities."

Elevating Quality:

Grammar and Style: Chat GBT are your vigilant proofreaders and style guides. They can ensure that your content not only adheres to grammatical rules but also matches your desired writing style, whether it's formal, casual, or technical.

Research Assistance: These AI models are research powerhouses. They sift through vast amounts of data to provide you with accurate and up-to-date information, saving you hours of manual research.

Example: You've written a research paper on climate change and need to improve its overall quality. You can instruct ChatGPT with this prompt: "Review my research paper on climate change. Provide suggestions for improving the organization of content, enhancing clarity, and ensuring it adheres to academic writing standards.

Personalization and Engagement:

Email Campaigns: Personalized email campaigns have a significantly higher engagement rate. With AI, you can create emails that address each recipient by name and tailor the content to their preferences, increasing the likelihood of conversions.

Tailored Recommendations: E-commerce platforms can use AI-generated product recommendations to boost sales. Chat GBT analyze user behavior and preferences to suggest products that match individual tastes, leading to higher customer satisfaction.

Example: You work for an online fashion retailer, and you're preparing personalized email recommendations for customers based on their browsing and purchase history. You can prompt ChatGPT with: "Generate individualized product recommendations for our customers. Incorporate their past purchases and preferences into the email content."

Efficiency and Productivity:

Content Generation at Scale: Whether you're running a news website or a data-driven business, these AI models can produce content at an impressive speed. They ensure that you stay ahead of the competition by delivering timely and relevant content.

Multilingual Content: In a globalized world, language should never be a barrier. Chat GBT are proficient in multiple languages, allowing you to expand your reach to international audiences effortlessly.

Example: You're managing a news website, and there's a breaking news story about a significant political event. You need to publish a news article quickly. You provide ChatGPT with this prompt: "Summarize the key points of the breaking news article on the political event and help me create a concise news update."

Collaboration and Brainstorming:

Teamwork: Writing often involves collaboration. These AI models facilitate brainstorming sessions, helping teams generate innovative ideas, create content outlines, and overcome writer's block collectively.

Example: Your marketing team is brainstorming ideas for a new advertising campaign for a fitness brand. You include ChatGPT in the discussion with this prompt: "Generate creative taglines, content ideas, and potential target audience demographics for our upcoming fitness brand advertising campaign."

Quality Control:

Proofreading and Editing: AI is meticulous in proofreading and editing. It doesn't miss typos, grammatical errors, or style inconsistencies, ensuring that your content is polished and error-free.

Plagiarism Checks: In the academic world and content creation, originality is paramount. AI can scan content for plagiarism, giving you peace of mind that your work is unique and respects intellectual property.

Tone and Style Adjustments: AI fine-tunes content to match specific tones, styles, or brand guidelines, making it adaptable to your audience's preferences.

Example: You're a content creator responsible for producing social media posts for a fashion brand. Before scheduling posts, you use ChatGPT to review and edit the content. Your prompt can be: "Edit and proofread the following social media post to ensure it is error-free and maintains a consistent brand voice."

Versatility:

Tone and Style Adjustments: Whether you need content that's formal, conversational, persuasive, or informative, Chat GBT can adapt to your requirements. They ensure that your content resonates with your target audience.

Time Efficiency: In a fast-paced digital landscape, time is often the most precious resource. These AI models allow you to generate content quickly and efficiently, meeting tight deadlines without compromising on quality.

Incorporating Chat GBT into your content creation process isn't just about automation; it's about elevating the entire creative journey. These AI companions are poised to redefine how we write, offering efficiency, personalization, and quality that were once unimaginable. As we explore their capabilities further, you'll discover how they're reshaping industries and empowering content creators worldwide.

Example: You're a technical writer working on a user manual for a software product. You need ChatGPT to generate clear and concise instructions. Your prompt is: "Create step-by-step instructions for users on how to install and configure our software product. Please ensure a technical and precise tone.

Email Marketing

Email marketing is a powerful tool for engaging with customers and prospects. ChatGPT can enhance your email marketing efforts in several ways:

Personalized Email Content: ChatGPT can generate personalized email content based on user data and preferences. For example, if you have an e-commerce platform, it can help you create product recommendations tailored to each subscriber's browsing and purchase history, increasing the likelihood of conversions.

Automated Responses: ChatGPT can handle automated responses to customer inquiries and support requests via email. It can provide quick answers to frequently asked questions, improving response times and customer satisfaction.

A/B Testing: ChatGPT can assist in crafting A/B test email variations. It can generate different subject lines, email body content, and calls to action, allowing you to determine which version performs better in terms of open rates and click-through rates.

Content Ideas: If you're running a content-rich newsletter, ChatGPT can suggest ideas for newsletter articles, blog posts, and other content. It can help you maintain a consistent publishing schedule and keep subscribers engaged.

Segmentation: ChatGPT can analyze your subscriber list and segment it based on various criteria such as demographics, behavior, and preferences. This segmentation enables you to send targeted and relevant emails to specific audience segments.

Subject Lines and Preheaders: ChatGPT can generate compelling subject lines and preheaders to increase email open rates. It can analyze trends in your industry and audience preferences to craft attention-grabbing subject lines.

Social Media Engagement

Social media is a dynamic platform for connecting with your audience. ChatGPT can be a valuable asset for social media management:

Content Creation: ChatGPT can help you generate social media captions, hashtags, and post content. Whether you're posting daily updates or launching a social media campaign, it can ensure your content is engaging and relevant.

Response Automation: ChatGPT can automate responses to user comments and messages on social media platforms. It can provide timely replies to common queries, improving customer support and community management.

Crisis Management: In the event of a social media crisis or negative comments, ChatGPT can assist in crafting appropriate responses to address the situation professionally and effectively.

By incorporating ChatGPT into your email marketing and social media strategies, you can streamline processes, enhance personalization, and improve overall engagement with your audience. These AI-powered capabilities offer a competitive edge in the digital marketing landscape, allowing you to connect with your customers on a deeper level and drive better results.

Academic Writing and Research

Literature Review: ChatGPT serves as a valuable assistant for researchers when conducting literature reviews. Instead of manually sifting through numerous academic papers and books, researchers can utilize ChatGPT to generate concise summaries, identify research gaps, and synthesize key findings. It's like having a research assistant who never asks for coffee breaks or vacations! Whether you're exploring the historical development of quantum physics or dissecting the nuances of Victorian literature, ChatGPT has your back with insightful insights.

Idea Generation: Research often begins with a spark of inspiration, and ChatGPT can help ignite these ideas. Researchers can engage with ChatGPT to brainstorm research topics, formulate hypotheses, and explore creative avenues for their studies. It's similar to having a brainstorming session with a witty AI friend who always has intriguing ideas up its digital sleeve. From contemplating the mysteries of dark matter to unraveling the complexities of human behavior, ChatGPT is your partner in intellectual exploration.

Thesis and Dissertation Writing: ChatGPT can be an invaluable companion for graduate students working on their theses or dissertations. It assists in various aspects of academic writing, including structuring chapters, generating clear and concise explanations, and maintaining a consistent writing style throughout your magnum opus.

Citation and Referencing: Maintaining accurate and consistent citations and references is crucial in academic writing. ChatGPT simplifies this process by helping researchers format citations and references in different styles, such as APA, MLA, or Chicago. It's like having a personal citation butler who ensures your sources are always properly dressed for the occasion. No more wrestling with citation manuals; ChatGPT handles the details while you focus on your research.

Statistical Analysis Interpretation: Research often involves complex statistical analyses, and ChatGPT can assist researchers in interpreting the results. It deciphers statistical jargon and provides meaningful explanations, making your data comprehensible and actionable. From t-tests to regression analyses, ChatGPT is your statistical companion.

Research Proposal Writing: Crafting a compelling research proposal is essential for securing funding or gaining approval for a research project. ChatGPT aids researchers in preparing comprehensive research proposals, guiding you through the process of outlining objectives, justifying the research's significance, and detailing the methodology. It's equivalent to a persuasive speechwriter who knows how to charm funding agencies and review committees.

Data Analysis Guidance: ChatGPT offers guidance on selecting appropriate data analysis techniques and tools, ensuring that your research questions are answered effectively. It's as if you have a GPS for data analysis, ensuring you take the right statistical turns on your research journey. Whether you're conducting surveys, experiments, or observational studies, ChatGPT helps you navigate the statistical terrain.

Academic Writing Tips: ChatGPT serves as a writing coach, providing tips and recommendations to improve academic writing style and clarity. It suggests ways to enhance the coherence of your arguments, refine your vocabulary, and structure your papers for maximum impact. It simulates a personal writing guru who polishes your prose to perfection. Your research papers will not only impress your professors but also engage your readers.

Research Paper Editing: Ensuring that research papers adhere to grammar and style guidelines is crucial for publication. ChatGPT can act as a meticulous proofreader and editor, catching grammar mistakes, improving sentence structure, and enhancing overall readability. It can be eagle-eyed editor who spots typos faster than you can say "peer rcvicw." Your papers will shine with academic brilliance.

Literature Search: Conducting extensive literature searches is a fundamental part of academic research. ChatGPT assists researchers in finding relevant sources by generating lists of academic articles, journals, and books related to their research topics. It's like having a research librarian who never shushes you and always finds the right book. ChatGPT brings the library to your screen, saving you hours of scrolling through databases.

Language Translation

Language Barriers

Language is a powerful tool for communication, but it can also be a barrier, hindering effective interaction between individuals who speak different languages. In a globally connected world, the ability to overcome these language barriers is crucial for businesses, travelers, and anyone seeking to engage with a diverse audience.

This is where ChatGPT steps in as a versatile language translation assistant. It leverages its language capabilities to provide accurate and context-aware translations between multiple languages, making it an invaluable resource for various scenarios:

Business Expansion: For businesses looking to expand into international markets, ChatGPT can assist in translating marketing materials, product descriptions, and customer communications. This ensures that the message resonates with local audiences and enhances the chances of success in foreign markets.

Multilingual Content Creation: Content creators, bloggers, and social media influencers often aim to reach a global audience. ChatGPT helps in translating blog posts, social media captions, and content for websites, allowing creators to engage with readers from different linguistic backgrounds.

Travel and Tourism: Travelers can use ChatGPT as a handy travel companion. It can translate signs, menus, and conversations in real-time, making navigation in foreign countries more accessible and enjoyable.

Cross-Cultural Communication: In multicultural workplaces or international collaborations, ChatGPT facilitates communication by translating emails, documents, and messages accurately. This fosters better understanding and cooperation among team members.

Language Learning: Language learners benefit from ChatGPT's ability to provide translations, explanations, and vocabulary assistance. It can assist in understanding complex phrases and idiomatic expressions in a foreign language.

Academic Research: Researchers can use ChatGPT to translate foreign-language research papers and articles, ensuring they have access to a broader range of academic sources for their studies.

Example: Imagine you're a small e-commerce business owner based in the United States, and you want to expand your reach to Spanish-speaking customers in Latin America. You can use ChatGPT to translate your product listings and website content into Spanish, making it more accessible to your target audience and potentially boosting sales in the region.

Incorporating ChatGPT into language translation tasks not only saves time but also enhances the quality and accuracy of translations. Its ability to understand context and nuances in language ensures that the translated content feels natural and resonates with the intended audience. Whether it's for business, travel, education, or cross-cultural communication, ChatGPT is your reliable partner in breaking down language barriers and fostering global connections.

How to use Chat Gbt

Step 1: Accessing ChatGPT

- **Visit OpenAI's Website**: Use your web browser to navigate to OpenAI's official website or directly to the ChatGPT interface if it's hosted on a separate page.

- **Login or Sign Up**: If you already have an account, log in with your credentials. If not, you will need to sign up for an account by providing your email address and creating a password.

Step 2: Familiarizing with the Interface

- **Explore the Dashboard**: Once logged in, take a moment to familiarize yourself with the interface. You will typically see a chatbox where you can type your prompts and a history of your past interactions.

Step 3: Starting a Session

- **Enter Your Prompt**: In the chatbox, type in your prompt or question. Your prompt can be anything from a specific question to a request for a piece of creative writing.

- **Submit Your Prompt**: Press the 'Enter' key or click on the 'Send' button to submit your prompt to ChatGPT.

Step 4: Receiving and Refining Responses

- **Review the Response**: ChatGPT will process your input and provide a response in the chat interface. Read through the response to see if it meets your requirements.

- **Refine Your Prompt**: If the response isn't quite what you were looking for, you can refine your prompt to be more specific, provide additional context, or ask follow-up questions.

Step 5: Iterating and Experimenting

- **Iterate as Needed**: Don't hesitate to continue the conversation with ChatGPT by asking more questions or requesting clarifications to get the information or content that you need.

- **Experiment with Different Prompts**: Try out different types of prompts to explore the capabilities of ChatGPT. You can ask for jokes, stories, explanations, code, and much more.

Step 6: Using Advanced Features (if available)

- **Explore Plugins**: If the interface has plugins, you can use them to enhance ChatGPT's capabilities. This might include translating languages, solving math problems, or integrating with other software.

Step 7: Ending Your Session

- **Logout**: Once you are done, you can log out of your session for security, especially if you are using a shared or public computer.
- **Save Your Work**: If you need to keep a record of your conversation, make sure to save it. Some interfaces have an export option, or you could simply copy and paste the conversation into a document.

Step 8: Reviewing and Applying the Output

- **Review the Generated Text**: Evaluate the text generated by ChatGPT to ensure it fulfills your intended purpose.
- **Apply the Output**: Use the text as needed for your project, whether it's content for a website, material for a presentation, or ideas for a creative piece.

ChatGPT is a versatile tool that can assist you with a wide array of text generation needs. By following this step-by-step guide, you can maximize the utility of ChatGPT and integrate its AI-powered capabilities into your workflow efficiently. Remember that the more specific and detailed your prompts are, the better the AI can generate responses that meet your needs.

The Power of Plugins - Amplifying ChatGPT's Abilities

In the digital age where AI tools like ChatGPT are revolutionizing how we work and create, plugins play a pivotal role in enhancing these capabilities. The marketplace is teeming with an ever-growing array of plugins, with new and innovative options being released frequently. These plugins serve as extensions that can significantly expand the functionality of AI tools, allowing them to be customized for a wide range of tasks and workflows. As you explore some of the most engaging plugins available, remember that experimentation can lead to discovery. You are encouraged to try out various plugins, combine their features, and find the set that best aligns with your unique requirements, ultimately enriching your interaction with AI technology.

Copart: The Thrifty Assistant

Utility: Copart is like a digital bargain hunter, tirelessly scouring the internet to find the best deals and the most valuable coupon codes.

Advanced Application: It's not just for casual shopping; businesses can leverage Copart to cut costs on software subscriptions, office supplies, and even enterprise services. It's like having a financial advisor who ensures you never miss a chance to save.

Wolfram Plugin: The Omniscient Oracle

Capabilities: This plugin is like having access to a vast, digital brain. It can process and provide data on a range of topics from meteorological to mathematical, pulling from a comprehensive database with computational power.

Enhanced Usage: It's particularly useful for interactive learning environments, data analysis in professional settings, or even settling debates with its vast knowledge base. From calculating complex formulas to providing historical data, it serves as a real-time research assistant.

EDX: The Academic Archive

Purpose: EDX connects curious minds to a repository of courses from top-tier universities, turning the internet into a virtual campus.

Extended Use Case: It's a resource not just for students, but also for professionals seeking to upskill, hobbyists looking to explore new fields, or educators seeking to supplement their curriculum with high-quality content.

One Word Domain: The Brand Builder

Function: One Word Domain simplifies the process of securing a digital identity by finding and comparing domain name availability and prices.

Strategic Example: For startups and brands, it's a tool to carve out a niche online, securing a domain that aligns with brand identity and ensuring they have a memorable and impactful online presence.

Tasty: The Culinary Companion

Feature: Tasty brings a smorgasbord of recipes, meal plans, and cooking advice to your digital table, drawing from a database brimming with culinary inspiration.

Robust Application: It's a boon for food bloggers, culinary students, or anyone planning a dinner party who wants to explore new dishes or refine their cooking techniques.

Web Pilot: The Content Curator

Functionality: Web Pilot navigates the vast seas of online content to generate articles and summaries from existing web pages.

Dynamic Use Case: Ideal for content marketers, educators, or anyone in need of quickly creating educational or promotional material. It can distill information from comprehensive sources into digestible content.

Vox Script: The Data Diver

Capabilities: Vox Script is like a virtual librarian, fetching transcripts, financial figures, and search result data from various online sources.

Practical Example: Journalists, market analysts, or content creators can use it to gather background information, statistical data, or quotes to bolster their articles, reports, or presentations.

Travel Deals with Kayak and Expedia: The Voyager's Vantage

Functionality: This plugin searches for cost-effective travel options, finding the best deals on accommodations and flights.

Advanced Example: For travel agencies or personal travel planners, it's a tool to construct detailed itineraries that offer the best value for clients, streamlining the planning process.

AI Diagram: The Visual Storyteller

Feature: Diagram enables users to create and edit complex diagrams within ChatGPT, transforming abstract concepts into clear visual representations.

Sophisticated Use Case: Invaluable for educators creating teaching aids, business analysts presenting data, or developers mapping out software architecture. It simplifies the translation of complex ideas into understandable visuals.

Zapier Plugin: The Efficiency Expert

Utility: This plugin automates tasks across different apps and platforms, creating a web of connections that streamline workflows.

Comprehensive Example: Perfect for project managers integrating project updates into communication channels or for sales teams syncing leads and customer interactions across CRM systems.

Ask Your PDF Plugin: The Digital Detective

Function: It turns static PDF documents into an interactive, searchable database.

In-Depth Usage: Researchers can dive into extensive reports to extract specific data points, legal professionals can search for precedents in case files, and students can study and interact with educational materials.

Video Insights Plugin: The Visual Analyst

Capabilities: This plugin provides a thorough breakdown of video content, including detailed transcriptions and executive summaries.

Strategic Application: Media analysts, marketers, and educators can use this tool to quickly obtain transcriptions of videos for content analysis, accessibility conversion, or to distill the essence of long-form visual content into actionable insights.

The Evolution of AI Conversation: Bard and Bing Chat

In the panorama of AI conversational tools, ChatGPT has set a high standard. However, the field is dynamic, with significant contributions from other tech giants such as Google and Microsoft. Now we'll compare Google Bard and Microsoft Bing Chat, offering insights into their functionalities, ease of use, and how they stand out in the AI landscape.

Google Bard: The AI Assistant with a Google Touch

Google Bard is conceived as a virtual companion adept at facilitating daily tasks. It's an AI-powered conversational tool that aims to bring creativity and efficiency to problem-solving, question-answering, and idea generation.

Accessing Google Bard: Utilizing Google Bard is straightforward: users visit bard.google.com and sign in using a personal Gmail account. It's important to note that Google Bard is tailored for personal use, not for professional Google Workspace accounts.

Setting Up a Google Account: For those new to Google's ecosystem, setting up a personal account is the first step. The process is user-centric, requiring basic personal information, a secure password, and agreement to Google's privacy terms.

Using Google Bard: Google Bard presents a chat-like interface, reminiscent of conversational messaging platforms, which is intuitive for users. It offers the ability to reset conversations, view past interactions, and access updates and FAQs about the tool.

Interacting with Bard: Interaction is versatile: users can choose from Bard's suggested prompts or input their own. The AI processes these inputs and returns responses that range from concise overviews to comprehensive lists, tips, and synthesized conclusions.

Features and Tools in Bard: Bard comes equipped with interactive features such as feedback buttons, response export options, and the 'Google It' button for extended searches, alongside options to view alternative drafts for a well-rounded perspective.

Example Use Cases: Bard excels at generating creative content, such as blog post outlines and detailed travel itineraries, showcasing its capability to produce structured and informative content.

Verifying Information: A standout feature of Bard is the inclusion of source links in its responses, empowering users to verify the information directly, adding a layer of transparency and trustworthiness to its outputs.

Google Integration: The 'Google It' feature embeds Bard seamlessly into the broader Google ecosystem, streamlining the user's experience from AI-generated content to extended research on Google.

Microsoft Bing Chat: The AI that Knows the Web

Introduction to Microsoft Bing Chat: Microsoft's Bing Chat marries the extensive knowledge base of Bing's search capabilities with the conversational finesse of OpenAI's ChatGPT, offering a unique blend of AI chatbot functionality.

Accessing Bing Chat: Access to Bing Chat is currently offered to users who join a waitlist, signaling Microsoft's phased approach to rolling out the service. A Microsoft account is the key to unlocking Bing Chat's capabilities.

Using Bing Chat: Bing Chat extends the traditional search experience, allowing users to pose questions and receive detailed, AI-generated answers complete with citations, reflecting Microsoft's emphasis on transparency and source reliability.

Interactive Conversations: Bing Chat can handle a continuous stream of interaction, maintaining context and adapting its responses to ensure a coherent conversation.

Complex Queries and Creative Prompts: Whether it's practical queries or creative brainstorming, Bing Chat is equipped to deal with a variety of requests, from generating content ideas to assisting with specific dietary meal plans.

Microsoft Edge Integration: Bing Chat is tightly integrated with the Microsoft Edge browser, enhancing the user experience by providing the ability to interact with the AI without leaving the webpage they are browsing.

Compose Feature in Edge: The 'Compose' feature in Edge is a testament to Bing Chat's versatility, aiding users in generating content drafts tailored to their needs, whether for social media posts or professional blogs.

Limitations and User Experience: Bing Chat imposes a limit on interactions per thread but counters this with human-like response quality, aiming for a balance between practicality and user engagement.

As we continue on the journey through the world of AI-driven text generation, we recognize that these tools have not just altered the landscape of content creation; they have expanded it into new dimensions. AI text generation, exemplified by platforms like ChatGPT, Google Bard, Microsoft Bing Chat, and others, has proven to be a transformative force, offering unparalleled opportunities for efficiency, creativity, and personalization.

AI text generation has democratized the ability to create. No longer are individuals required to possess advanced writing skills to produce content; with AI, anyone can bring ideas to life through text. This technology has opened doors for entrepreneurs, educators, students, and creatives to generate written content that might otherwise have been beyond their reach.

But with great power comes great responsibility. The convenience and capabilities of AI text generation necessitate a conversation about its responsible use. As users, it is incumbent upon us to use these tools ethically, to check the accuracy of AI-generated content, and to credit AI contributions where appropriate.

IMAGE GENERATION WITH AI

Welcome to the exciting world of image creation, where the only thing you need to make art is an idea. In the old days, creating a picture could take years of learning and a lot of trial and error with brushes and paints. But now, there's a new way to make images that's changing everything. It's called Generative AI, and it's like having a superpower for art.

Think of Generative AI as a helpful friend who's really good at drawing. You just say what you're thinking—like "a cozy cabin in a snowy forest"—and before you know it, there's a beautiful picture right in front of you. It feels a bit like magic, but it's actually all about smart computers that understand how to turn words into pictures.

In this chapter, we're going to learn all about how this works. We'll look at the clever tricks these computers use to make images, check out the tools that let you do it yourself, and even think about some big questions, like what this all means for the future of making art.

No matter if you've been making art for a long time or if you just love looking at cool pictures, Generative AI is something you can get excited about. It's a new way to express yourself, to bring your ideas to life, and to have a lot of fun along the way.

The Mechanics of AI-Driven Image Generation: A Beginner's Guide

Creating images with generative AI is like telling a story to a painter who has never picked up a brush but can paint masterpieces instantly. It's fascinating, a little bit mysterious, and full of possibilities. Let's break down this process into simpler pieces and walk through some practical examples.

How Does It Work?

Imagine you're playing a game of 'draw this' with a computer. You say, "I want a picture of a cat," and the computer, with its AI, starts drawing. But how does the AI know what a cat looks like?

1. **Understanding through Learning**: The AI has been shown thousands, maybe millions, of pictures of cats. It doesn't just see the images; it looks for patterns—where the ears are, how the fur looks, the shape of the eyes. It's learning what makes a cat a cat.

2. **Creating Something New**: When you ask for a picture of a cat, the AI uses what it's learned to draw a new cat. It's not copying any picture it's seen before; it's using its 'knowledge' to make a brand new image.

Practical Example: Let's say you ask the AI for a picture of a cat wearing a wizard hat. The AI takes what it knows about cats and hats, mixes that all up, and draws a cat with a pointy hat, maybe with stars on it, looking like it's ready to cast a spell.

Training the AI

Training an AI is like teaching someone a skill, except you're teaching the computer.

1. **Feeding Data**: You start by giving the AI lots of pictures and information. This is its learning material, just like textbooks for students.
2. **Learning Patterns**: The AI goes through all this data and looks for patterns. It's figuring out things like, "Oh, this is what trees look like," or "This is how people stand."

Practical Example: You're training an AI to draw cars. You feed it images of different car models. Over time, the AI learns the basics: cars have wheels, windows, and doors. Then, it learns finer details: sports cars have sleek lines, trucks are bulkier, and so on.

Making the Image

When you're ready to create, you tell the AI what you want.

1. **Giving Instructions**: You give the AI a description, known as a 'prompt.' It's like telling an artist what to paint.
2. **The AI Works Its Magic**: The AI uses its training to interpret your prompt and starts creating the image.

Practical Example: You tell the AI, "Draw me a futuristic city at night." The AI remembers the patterns it learned from pictures of cities and nightscapes. It combines them to create a new image with glowing buildings, flying cars, and a dark sky full of stars.

Getting It Just Right

The first draft might not be perfect. That's where feedback comes in.

1. **Refining the Output**: You look at the picture and tell the AI what you like or don't like. "Make the buildings taller," or "Add more stars in the sky."
2. **AI Adapts**: The AI takes your feedback and adjusts the image accordingly. It's a back-and-forth process, a collaboration between you and the AI.

Practical Example: The AI's first version of your futuristic city has cars that look too much like today's cars. You tell the AI, "Make the cars look more high-tech." The AI then redraws the cars with a sleeker, more advanced design.

DALL-E - The Dawn of AI-Driven Imagination

In the evolving narrative of artificial intelligence, DALL-E emerges as a pivotal character, marking a renaissance in the way we think about and create images. Let's explore the history, capabilities, and practical use of this groundbreaking tool.

The Genesis of DALL-E

DALL-E's story began with a team of researchers at OpenAI, who unveiled it to the world as a system capable of generating images from textual descriptions, a process akin to sketching the words of a story. Named whimsically after the surrealist artist Salvador Dalí and the adorable robot WALL-E, DALL-E was designed to bridge the gap between art and AI, turning textual whims into visual realities.

Features and Capabilities

Imagination at Scale: DALL-E is not just a tool; it's a digital artist with an infinite palette. Its ability to understand and interpret text prompts allows it to create images that range from the realistic to the fantastically absurd.

Combinatorial Creativity: DALL-E excels at combining disparate elements. Ask for a "zebra with the wings of a butterfly," and it creates a hybrid creature that respects the anatomy of both.

Style and Substance: It can mimic styles, whether you want an image that looks like a watercolor painting or a pixel art from a video game.

Editing Reality: DALL-E can also take an existing image and make logical edits, like "add a hat to the person in the photo" or "turn this day scene into night."

How to Use DALL-E: A Step-by-Step Guide

Step 1: Accessing DALL-E

- Begin by visiting the OpenAI website and navigating to the DALL-E page. If it's your first time, you'll need to create an account. For returning users, simply log in.

Step 2: Crafting Your Prompt

- Think about what you want to create. Be as detailed as possible. Instead of "a bird," try "a parrot with the colors of a rainbow sitting on a branch in a dense jungle."

Step 3: Letting DALL-E Work Its Magic

- Enter your prompt into the text box provided. Hit the 'generate' button and give DALL-E a moment to process your request.

Step 4: Reviewing and Refining

- DALL-E will present you with several image options. Review them and decide if one matches your vision.
- If you're not satisfied, consider refining your prompt for clarity or specificity, and generate again.

Step 5: Downloading Your Creation

- Once you're happy with an image, you can download it. Depending on the platform's rules, you may use it for personal projects, share it on social media, or even incorporate it into commercial work.

Bringing Your Visions to Life

DALL-E's capabilities are not just a leap forward in AI technology; they represent a democratization of creativity. With DALL-E, artists and non-artists alike can bring their inner visions to visual life, bypassing the steep learning curve of traditional art skills.

The Ongoing Evolution

As with any technology, DALL-E continues to evolve. Its newer versions promise even more precision and creative freedom, suggesting a future where our visual imaginations are limited only by the language we use to describe them.

Midjourney into Visual Imagination

Continuing lto unravel the tapestry of AI image generation tools, Midjourney stands out with its own distinct thread. Midjourney may not be as widely recognized as DALL-E, but it's a tool that deserves attention for its unique approach to crafting images from the abstract lanes of thought.

Navigating Midjourney: A Detailed Look

Midjourney, an AI image generation tool, offers a unique blend of creative exploration and technological innovation. Let's delve deeper into its features and how they facilitate a nuanced approach to image generation.

Diverse Initial Outputs

One of the standout features of Midjourney is its approach to initial image generation. Unlike tools that provide a single result, Midjourney presents four different images in response to your prompt. This variety is key to its explorative nature.

- **Multiple Perspectives**: When you input a prompt, Midjourney generates four distinct interpretations. For instance, if your prompt is "a futuristic city," you'll receive four different visions of what that could look like, each with unique elements and atmospheres.
- **Wide Range of Inspirations**: These varying outputs encourage you to think broadly and consider different possibilities. You might find elements in one image that you love and aspects in another you want to explore further.

Iterative Refinement

Midjourney is designed for iteration. Once you have your initial set of images, the journey truly begins.

- **Selection and Expansion**: From the four options, you can choose one to refine further. This choice tells Midjourney which direction you're interested in exploring.
- **Detailing Your Vision**: After selecting an image, you can ask Midjourney to elaborate on it. This can mean enhancing the resolution, zooming in on a specific area, or adjusting certain elements based on your feedback.

Collaborative Creativity

Midjourney emphasizes the collaborative aspect of AI and human interaction. It's not just about commanding the AI, it's about working with it.

- **Feedback Loop**: As you interact more with Midjourney, providing feedback and making selections, the AI learns from your preferences. Over time, it becomes more attuned to your style and the nuances of what you're looking for in your images.

- **Creative Partnership**: This process turns Midjourney into a creative partner, one that understands your preferences and offers visual suggestions that align with your artistic vision.

Stylistic Versatility

The ability of Midjourney to adapt to various artistic styles is another of its impressive features.

- **Style Mimicking**: Whether you want an image that looks like a classic oil painting or a modern digital art piece, Midjourney can adjust its outputs to mimic these styles.
- **Incorporating Artistic Influences**: You can even guide Midjourney to create images in the vein of specific artists or art movements, adding another layer of customization to your creations.

User-Driven Evolution

Finally, Midjourney's evolution is significantly influenced by its user base.

- **Community Input**: User feedback and interactions play a crucial role in shaping how Midjourney evolves. The tool 'learns' from the collective creative input of its community.
- **Ongoing Development**: This means that Midjourney is continuously improving, not just in terms of image quality but also in understanding and interpreting creative prompts.

VIDEO GENERATION WITH AI

As we turn the page from still images to the dynamic world of moving pictures, we enter the realm of video generation with AI. This fascinating journey takes us beyond the static, breathing life into our visual stories with motion and time. Video generation with AI is not just an extension of image generation; it's a whole new dimension of creativity, where the stillness of pictures is transformed into the fluidity of narrative.

The Magic of Movement

Imagine being able to create a video from a simple description, just like how AI image generators craft pictures from text prompts. But now, it's not just about a single frame; it's about a sequence, a story unfolding over time. AI in video generation does this by understanding and predicting motion, creating seamless transitions from one frame to the next.

The Power of AI in Video

AI video generation tools are like having a director, cinematographer, and editor all rolled into one intelligent system. They can create videos from scratch, manipulate existing footage, or combine elements of both to produce something entirely new.

A New Era of Storytelling

With AI-assisted video creation, the barriers to filmmaking and animation are lowered. No longer is video production confined to those with extensive resources or technical skills. AI opens up a world where anyone with a story can bring it to life, whether it's for personal expression, business communication, or entertainment.

Applications and Possibilities

This technology has wide-ranging applications, from creating short films or animations to generating realistic simulations for training and education. Marketers can craft engaging content, educators can bring lessons to life, and artists can experiment with new forms of visual storytelling.

What Lies Ahead

Continuing to delve into the intricacies of video generation with AI, we will discover how these tools work, explore various platforms offering these capabilities, and look at practical examples of how they're being used.

The world of AI video generation is not just about technology; it's about the dreams and ideas that can be brought to life. It's a journey into a future where our stories are not just told but are vividly shown, where our imaginations are not just pictured but are set in motion.

The Role of Machine Learning in AI-Driven Video Generation

Machine learning (ML) models specifically designed for video play a pivotal role in AI-driven video generation. These models are sophisticated pieces of technology that require extensive training to perform their tasks effectively. Let's go trough the intricacies of their role.

Training the AI for Motion Understanding

- **Data Ingestion**: ML models begin their education by ingesting a vast library of videos, encompassing everything from simple movements to complex interactions. This library is not just a collection of random clips but a curated dataset that represents a wide variety of scenarios, objects, and actions.

- **Pattern Recognition**: As the AI processes these videos, it uses algorithms to identify and understand patterns of motion, like a child learning through observation, recognizing how certain actions lead to predictable outcomes.
- **Contextual Learning**: The AI is trained to understand context—a cat jumping off a couch lands differently than a squirrel leaping between trees. This context-specific learning is crucial for generating realistic movements in videos.

Interpolation: Filling in the Motion Gaps

- **Keyframe Analysis**: Keyframes are significant frames within a video that represent important positions or moments of transition. AI analyzes these to understand the 'story' of movement.
- **Motion Prediction**: Between keyframes, AI predicts intermediary frames. This involves calculating the trajectory and velocity of moving objects and understanding how they interact with their environment.
- **In-Between Generation**: Like an animator who draws the main frames and then fills in the gaps, AI generates 'in-betweens' to bridge keyframes, creating a smooth sequence.

Creating Continuity in AI-Generated Videos

Maintaining continuity is essential for the believability and coherence of a video. AI uses several techniques to ensure that videos flow smoothly from frame to frame.

- **Temporal Coherence**: AI examines the sequence of frames to ensure that each new frame is a logical follow-up to the last. This isn't just about objects moving smoothly but also about maintaining narrative consistency throughout the video.
- **Consistency Checks**: The AI performs checks to ensure that characters and objects behave and appear consistently throughout the video. For example, if a character starts out wearing a red shirt, the AI ensures the shirt doesn't inexplicably change color or style midway through the video.
- **Error Correction**: When the AI detects inconsistencies, it employs error correction algorithms to adjust future frames, preserving the continuity of both the narrative and the visuals.

Style Consistency Across AI-Generated Video Frames

Style consistency is particularly important when the AI-generated video needs to mimic a specific artistic style or maintain a brand's aesthetic.

- **Style Encoding**: The AI encodes stylistic elements from the training data and learns to apply these stylistic features consistently across all generated frames.
- **Adaptive Styling**: If the AI is prompted to change the video style mid-generation—say from a realistic to a cartoonish appearance—it adapts new frames to transition smoothly into the new style without abrupt changes.
- **Aesthetic Fine-Tuning**: For finer control, some AI systems allow users to fine-tune aesthetic elements like color saturation, contrast, and brightness to maintain a consistent style.

By mastering the roles of machine learning in motion understanding, interpolation, and maintaining continuity and style, AI-driven video generation is able to produce not just visually pleasing but also contextually coherent videos. These capabilities open up a new frontier for creators, where AI becomes an essential tool in the video production process, enabling the creation of content that was once impossible or prohibitively expensive to produce.

Runway ML – Pioneering AI-Assisted Creativity

Runway ML stands as a testament to the evolution of AI in the creative industry, offering a suite of tools that empower artists, designers, and creators of all kinds.

It emerged from the desire to democratize access to machine learning for creative projects. It was born out of the recognition that while machine learning had vast potential from a creative point of view, the barrier to entry was often too high for those without a technical background. Runway ML was designed to bridge this gap, making powerful AI tools accessible to anyone with a vision to create.

Runway ML's "Magic Tools"

Runway ML's "Magic Tools" are a suite of AI-powered features designed to streamline complex video and image editing processes, making them accessible to users without the need for in-depth technical knowledge. These tools use advanced machine learning algorithms to automate and enhance creative tasks. Here's an explanation of some of these standout features:

Text to video

This tool is essentially a storyteller that translates written narratives into moving visuals. When you input a text description, the AI analyzes it and synthesizes a video that depicts the described scene. For instance, if you type "A dog playing in a field on a sunny day," the tool generates a video of that exact scenario, complete with dynamic elements like the dog moving and the grass swaying in the breeze.

Video To Video

The video to video feature is akin to a style chameleon. It takes an existing video and alters its style based on a new prompt or set of visual instructions. This could mean changing a daytime scene to night, transforming a real-life video into an animated sequence, or applying various artistic filters to change the video's aesthetic.

Text to Image

With this feature, you can create detailed images from textual descriptions. It works similarly to text to video but focuses on crafting a single, static image. This is particularly useful for generating unique artworks, concept art, or visual aids. For example, "A futuristic cityscape with flying cars" would prompt the AI to generate an image that brings this futuristic vision to life.

Image to Image

Image to image leverages style transfer and other AI techniques to take an existing image and transform it according to a new prompt or style reference. This could be used to reimagine a photograph in the style of a famous painter or to see how a landscape might look under different weather conditions. The AI understands the content of the original image and applies the requested changes while preserving the integrity of the original composition.

Green Screen Without the Green Screen (Remove Video Background)

Traditionally, separating a subject from the background required a green screen and careful lighting. Runway ML's tool allows you to achieve this effect without any setup, removing the background from any video with just a few clicks.

Object Removal (Inpainting)

Inpainting is like a magic eraser for unwanted objects in your video. Whether it's a stray piece of trash on a landscape or an unintended person walking through a shot, Runway ML can remove it and fill in the space convincingly as if the object was never there.

Auto-Tracking for Effects and Annotations (Motion Tracking)

Motion tracking is a complex task that typically requires specialized software. Runway ML simplifies this by automatically tracking moving objects in a video, allowing you to attach text, annotations, or even other videos to those objects seamlessly.

Dynamic Effects and Filters

Runway ML provides a library of effects and filters that can be applied to videos to alter their look and feel. These range from color adjustments and artistic filters to more complex effects like glitch or dreamy sequences.

Professional Color Grading

Color grading sets the tone and mood of a video. Runway ML's color grading tool uses AI to simplify the process, offering presets and controls that can give your video a specific emotional impact or visual style.

Text and Captioning

Adding text and captions is vital for accessibility and storytelling. Runway ML's text tools allow for easy insertion and customization of text over your videos, including adjusting fonts, colors, and timing.

Overlay Images or Videos

Overlays can add depth or context to a video. Runway ML lets you place images or secondary video clips over your primary footage, which is great for picture-in-picture effects or adding logos and watermarks.

Templates for Quick Editing

Templates are pre-designed video structures that you can customize with your content. Runway ML provides a variety of templates suited for different types of videos, such as social media posts, advertisements, or presentations.

Collaborative Editing

Runway ML allows multiple users to work on the same project in real-time, streamlining group projects and remote collaboration.

Audio Editing

Runway ML includes tools for adjusting and editing audio within your videos, allowing for a better match between the visual and auditory elements of your projects.

Export Options

Once your video is complete, Runway ML offers various export options, including different file formats and quality settings to suit your distribution needs.

AI-Powered Generative Tools

Runway ML incorporates cutting-edge AI models for tasks like creating images from text prompts (text-to-image), transforming images stylistically (image-to-image), expanding images beyond their original borders (expand image), and generating infinite variations of an image (infinite image).

These "Magic Tools" represent just a snapshot of Runway ML's capabilities, which continue to grow as the platform evolves. By leveraging AI, Runway ML is making sophisticated video and image editing tasks more accessible to creators of all skill levels.

Welcome to the revolutionary world of Runway Gen 1, a beta AI tool designed for the innovative generation of videos. This guide will walk you through the process of transforming ordinary footage into extraordinary AI-altered videos. Don't forget to engage with more AI content as you embark on this creative journey.

How to Use Runway Video to Video Tool Step-by-Step

Getting Started with Runway Gen 1

1. **Create Your Account**: Begin by signing up for Runway and accessing the Gen 1 beta version.

2. **Navigate to the Tool**: Once logged in, locate the 'Gen 1 video to video' feature within the Runway platform.

Preparing Your Video

1. **Capture Your Footage**: Record a video to serve as the base for your AI transformation. Consider the content of your video carefully, as it will influence the AI's alterations.

2. **Length Consideration**: Remember, Runway Gen 1 will use the first five seconds of your uploaded video, so plan your recording accordingly.

Uploading and Customizing Your Video in Runway

Upload Your Video: Import your recorded footage into Runway.

Adjust Style Strength: Modify the 'Style Strength' to set the intensity of AI alterations. A higher percentage results in more significant changes.

Choosing Your Generation Style

Try Various Styles: Runway Gen 1 offers several styles to choose from:

- **Text Prompts**: Input a descriptive text prompt for the AI to visualize. The more imaginative, the better—think "a noir detective in a rain-soaked city."

- **Preset Styles**: Select from Runway's preset styles, like "watercolor" or "claymation," for quick and themed transformations.

- **Image Assets**: Upload your own image for a personalized reference style or use Runway's demo assets for AI guidance.

Generating and Evaluating Your AI Video

Produce the Video: Command Runway to generate the video and then observe what it creates.

Assess the Outcome: Review the AI's work. It may not be flawless, and you'll likely notice some quirks and unexpected results, which are part of the AI's learning curve.

Refining Your Results

Review Different Styles: Evaluate how each style has impacted your video. Some may result in more realistic alterations, while others might present more abstract or artistic interpretations.

Consider Alternative Assets: If the initial results don't satisfy you, try different image assets or adjust your text prompts to guide the AI towards a more desirable outcome.

Exploring Advanced Features

Discover More on Runway: Dive deeper into the platform beyond the basic functions by exploring the Runway website, where you'll find a host of advanced settings. While exploring the advanced capabilities of Runway, it's also highly beneficial to experiment with the platform's other "Magic Tools". These tools represent the cutting edge of AI-driven creative technology and can significantly enhance your projects.

Synthesia: The Future of AI in Video Production

Picture a world where creating a professional video is as simple as writing an email. Synthesia makes this a reality. It's a platform that leverages AI to produce synthetic media, focusing on crafting realistic digital avatars and automated video content. This technology is a game-changer, especially for businesses and educators, offering a quick and cost-effective alternative to traditional video production methods.

AI-Powered Avatars

Synthesia's AI-Generated Avatars: More than mere digital creations, Synthesia's avatars are equal to sophisticated actors captured in silicon. They are programmed to exhibit a range of emotions and behaviors, closely mimicking human expressions and mannerisms. This is achieved through advanced AI algorithms that analyze and replicate human gestures and facial movements, making the avatars not just speak but communicate effectively.

> **Lifelike Presentations**: These avatars can take any script and breathe life into it. They can express joy, concern, surprise, and a multitude of other emotions, ensuring that the message isn't just delivered, but felt. This emotional connection is vital in conveying complex ideas or engaging with audiences on a more personal level.
>
> **Multilingual Marvels**: Synthesia's avatars are polyglots, capable of speaking in numerous languages and dialects. This feature is a boon for global businesses and organizations looking to connect with a diverse audience. From training videos to product demonstrations, these avatars can communicate in the local tongue, ensuring the message is not lost in translation.

Crafting Custom Content with Synthesia

Seamless Video Production: Synthesia has streamlined the video production process, allowing for the creation of high-quality content with minimal effort and technical know-how.

> **From Script to Screen**: The process begins with a script. Once entered into Synthesia, the AI takes over, animating the avatar to deliver the script. This technology eliminates the logistical challenges

of traditional video production, such as location scouting, lighting, and sound design, making professional video creation more accessible than ever.

A Palette of Personalization: Synthesia offers a wide array of customization options. You can choose the appearance of your avatar, from their clothing to their hair style, aligning with your brand or the tone of your message. The backgrounds aren't static either; whether you need a corporate setting, a casual café, or an abstract digital space, Synthesia can accommodate.

User-Friendly Interface: Designed with the user in mind, Synthesia's interface is intuitive, guiding you through each step of the creation process. This ease of use democratizes video production, empowering individuals and businesses to create content that would otherwise require specialized skills and equipment.

Practical Applications of Synthesia

A Tool for Various Industries: Synthesia's capabilities make it an invaluable tool across various sectors.

Corporate Training & E-Learning: In corporate settings, Synthesia can be used to create engaging training materials. AI avatars can act as instructors or guides, leading employees through complex processes or compliance training in a relatable and understandable way.

Marketing & Advertising: For marketing professionals, Synthesia offers a way to create unique and engaging content. Whether it's for social media campaigns, product launches, or brand storytelling, the ability to produce multilingual content adds a significant edge in reaching a broader audience.

Personalized Communication: Synthesia is also perfect for crafting personalized messages for special occasions, customer engagement, or community outreach. These custom videos can add a personal touch to digital communication, making interactions more memorable and impactful.

The world of AI-driven image and video creation is a dynamic and ever-expanding universe, teeming with possibilities. As creators, educators, marketers, and storytellers, we have at our disposal an incredible array of tools that can help turn our wildest imaginations into reality. The challenge and opportunity lie in harnessing these tools to create content that is not only visually stunning but also meaningful and impactful. By embracing these technologies, we step into a future where the only limit to creation is our imagination.

MUSIC CREATION WITH AI

Imagine a world where the melodies that once required a composer's intricate touch could spring forth from the digital mind of a computer. This is no longer the stuff of science fiction. It's the reality of today's music industry, thanks to the advent of AI music creation.

Artificial Intelligence is redefining the soundscape of our lives, infusing the music production process with a blend of algorithmic precision and creative flair. AI music creation involves sophisticated software that can compose, perform, and even respond to music in real-time. It is a field where technology meets art, leading to an exciting paradigm shift in how music is made.

AI doesn't just mimic existing musical styles; it can learn from vast collections of music and generate new compositions that resonate with the human soul. These AI systems are trained using machine learning algorithms, feeding on everything from classical symphonies to modern pop hits, learning the nuances of rhythm, harmony, and melody. They don't just understand music theory; they apply it in ways that can both imitate and innovate.

But AI in music isn't just about creating songs. It's about expanding the creative toolkit available to musicians, producers, and hobbyists. It offers a new way to experiment with sound, a fresh perspective on songwriting, and the ability to generate musical ideas that might otherwise never have been discovered.

As AI music creation tools become more accessible, they have the potential to democratize music production, allowing anyone with a passion for music to explore their creativity, regardless of their technical skill or theoretical knowledge. This technology can serve as a virtual collaborator, an endless source of inspiration, or even a music tutor.

However, this new era of AI-assisted music creation raises questions about the nature of artistry and creativity. What does it mean for a piece of music to be composed by an algorithm? How do we attribute value and copyright in the age of AI? These are just some of the challenges and discussions that accompany the integration of AI into the creative process.

As we begin this exploration of AI music creation, we'll investigate the technology's capabilities, the magic behind the algorithms, and the myriad ways in which it's being used. From the bedroom producer to the film composer, AI is opening up new range of possibilities, and the symphony it creates is only just beginning to unfold.

AI, Music Theory, and the Models that Learn

The integration of AI in music creation is a harmonious blend of data science and artistry. Now we'll explore how AI algorithms are trained on the foundational principles of music theory and vast datasets, and it delves into the specific AI models used in music creation.

Training AI on Music Theory

Data Collection: The Foundation of AI Music Training

The journey of an AI in music creation begins with an extensive data collection phase. The goal here is to gather a corpus that is as rich and varied as the global musical landscape:

- **Variety of Sources**: AI's understanding of music is built upon datasets collected from a variety of sources that include sheet music from classical masterpieces, jazz standards, folk songs, and contemporary pop hits.

- **Depth and Breadth**: The collection spans centuries of music composition, encapsulating the evolution of musical styles and preferences. It's not just about quantity but also the quality and diversity of data, ensuring the AI has a well-rounded exposure to different musical expressions.

- **Multidimensional Data**: Beyond the notes and melodies, this data encompasses various musical dimensions such as instrumentation, artist performances, and live recordings, providing a multi-faceted view of music.

Feature Extraction: Deciphering Musical DNA

In the feature extraction stage, AI algorithms dissect the collected data to identify and understand the core elements of music:

- **Pattern Recognition**: Using sophisticated algorithms, AI sifts through the datasets to detect recurring patterns and sequences in music, such as the common motifs found in baroque compositions or the syncopated beats characteristic of reggae.

- **Structural Analysis**: The AI examines the structure of compositions, learning how verses, choruses, bridges, and solos are typically assembled to create a complete piece of music.
- **Harmonic Analysis**: Algorithms parse chord progressions and harmonic relationships, gaining an understanding of how different chords can evoke particular emotions or musical tensions.
- **Rhythmic Understanding**: AI breaks down complex rhythmic patterns, grasping how different rhythms contribute to the overall feel of a musical genre, from the swing in jazz to the driving beats of electronic dance music.

Music Theory Principles: The Rulebook for AI Composers

AI models are then introduced to the theoretical frameworks that underpin musical compositions:

- **Scales and Modes**: The AI learns about different scales and modes, the building blocks of melody, and how they influence the mood and style of a piece.
- **Key and Time Signatures**: Understanding key signatures helps AI determine the tonal center of a piece, while time signatures provide the rhythmic foundation upon which rhythms are built.
- **Composition Rules**: AI is trained on the 'rules' of music theory, such as counterpoint in classical music or the 12-bar blues format, which dictate how melodies, harmonies, and rhythms interact in well-formed compositions.
- **Cultural Nuances**: The AI also learns about the cultural context of music, recognizing that certain scales or rhythms are indigenous to specific musical traditions and carry deep cultural significance.

Supervised Learning: The AI's Apprenticeship

During supervised learning, the AI is like an apprentice, learning from the masters through examples:

- **Labelled Datasets**: AI is provided with labelled examples, where it is given both the music (input) and the annotations (output), such as the key, tempo, or genre of a piece.
- **Feedback Loops**: Human experts often provide feedback, correcting the AI's mistakes and reinforcing correct patterns, much like a music teacher guiding a student.

- **Contextual Learning**: The AI begins to understand not just the music itself but also its context, learning that certain compositional techniques are more prevalent in specific eras or styles.
- **Learning Through Examples**: By analyzing thousands of pieces of labelled music, the AI starts to generalize and predict musical elements in new compositions, applying the learned principles to generate original music.

AI Models in Music Creation

Several AI models have risen to prominence in the field of music creation. These models vary in complexity and application:

The symphony of AI models in music creation is as intricate and diverse as the genres of music they seek to emulate and innovate. As we delve deeper into these models, we enter a realm where artificial intelligence becomes an architect of auditory experience, crafting soundscapes that resonate with both the logic of algorithms and the intuition of human emotion.

Recurrent Neural Networks (RNNs)

RNNs are the troubadours of the AI music world, spinning melodic yarns note by note. They excel in recognizing and predicting sequences, making them adept at composing melodies that follow a logical and emotionally resonant progression. Imagine a pianist who remembers each previous note played, allowing each subsequent note to flow in a way that feels intentional and expressive. RNNs bring this sequential understanding to AI music creation, weaving together notes that tell a story.

Long Short-Term Memory (LSTM)

LSTMs are the maestros of the AI ensemble, with an uncanny ability to hold onto musical themes over extended periods. Where a simple RNN excels in short motifs, LSTM networks are similar to classical composers, capable of developing complex, multi-movement pieces where themes introduced early on are revisited and evolved throughout the piece. Their strength lies in their capacity to remember and integrate these motifs over time, creating music that unfolds with a sense of narrative and development that echoes the great symphonies and operas of yore.

Transformers

Transformers, the virtuosos known for their linguistic prowess, have now turned their attention to the language of music. They approach compositions not as a sequence of individual notes but as a cohesive whole, an entire score to be understood in one gaze. This allows them to craft music with a sense of long-term structure and thematic coherence, much like a conductor who oversees not just the individual notes played by each instrument but the symphony as a collective entity. They are particularly suited for genres where the interplay of multiple instruments and voices must converge into a harmonious whole.

Variational Autoencoders (VAEs)

VAEs are the fusion chefs in the kitchen of music, mixing ingredients from various genres and styles to create novel concoctions. They can take a piece of music, distill its essence into a compact form, and then reconstruct it, sometimes adhering to the original recipe, other times introducing a twist. With VAEs, one can take the skeleton of a baroque piece and flesh it out with the textures of jazz, or distill a rock anthem to its core before dressing it in electronic beats.

Generative Adversarial Networks (GANs)

GANs operate within a fascinating adversarial dynamic, like two musicians in a call-and-response duel. One network generates new compositions, while the other critiques them, pushing the creator to produce work that is increasingly refined and realistic. This interplay is like a perpetual masterclass where the student continuously learns from the feedback, striving for compositions that not only sound pleasing but also feel genuinely inspired and authentic.

WaveNet

WaveNet stands as the virtuoso of vocal expression in the AI music domain. Developed by DeepMind, this model generates raw audio waveforms with a focus on capturing the nuances of natural sound. WaveNet's prowess lies in its ability to produce music—and speech—that rivals the expressiveness and dynamic variation found in human performances. From the subtle breathiness of a whispered verse to the robust timbre of a sung chorus, WaveNet brings a human-like quality to AI-generated audio, blurring the lines between artificial and organic sound production.

Each of these models represents a unique approach to the challenge of creating music through artificial means. They embody the convergence of computational power and musical tradition, offering tools that are not just about simulating the music of the past but about imagining the music of the future.

The Symphony of AI Music Creation Softwares

Picture yourself standing before a vibrant orchestra, each musician contributing their unique melody to create a harmonious composition. In the realm of AI music creation software, this orchestra comes to life through innovative platforms, each adding its distinct notes to the digital composition symphony.

Waveformer

Waveformer serves as the musical polyglot of the AI world. It interprets text-based prompts and weaves them into compositions spanning genres, from the rhythmic beats of Boom Bap Hip Hop to the ethereal sounds of Progressive Instrumental House. While the output may carry some digital quirks, like a musician's individuality, it's a captivating fusion of linguistic input and musical output.

Strengths: Waveformer shows promise in bridging the gap between textual descriptions and genre-specific compositions.

Limitations: The presence of these quirks suggests room for refinement to achieve a cleaner sound, but even virtuoso musicians have their unique style.

Suno AI

Suno AI takes center stage by extending its capabilities to Discord, the social media platform.

Accessibility: Its integration with Discord makes it an excellent tool for collaborative and community-driven music creation, transforming your server into a virtual music studio.

Performance: The AI impresses with its ability to generate complete songs, although there's room for improvement in audio fidelity. It's like having a talented musician who sometimes adds a touch of spontaneity.

Wave Tool:

Wave Tool brings music creation right into your web browser, offering an interface that feels like home for experienced digital audio workstation (DAW) users.

User Experience: The DAW-like interface makes it approachable for those with experience in music production, providing a familiar environment.

Creativity: While the outputs are described as basic, the tool provides a fun and accessible way for users to experiment with AI-generated music.

Boomi:

Boomi is all about customization, offering a robust platform for crafting music in popular styles like Rap Beats and Boom Bap. With features for vocal additions and instrument rearrangement, it provides a hands-on creative experience.

Customization: Boomi's strength lies in its customization options, empowering you to tailor your tracks as you see fit.

Flexibility: The platform supports various musical styles and user input, promoting a versatile music-making experience.

Soundful:

Soundful offers a curated selection of templated tracks spanning a spectrum of genres. The sound quality is top-notch, although the software imposes some limits on customization.

Quality: The high sound quality of the templates makes Soundful a strong choice for ready-to-use tracks.

Range: Despite its strengths, the platform could benefit from expanding its customization features to foster greater creative freedom. Think of it as a finely crafted piece of music art.

Beethoven.ai:

Beethoven.ai is the virtuoso of royalty-free music, offering a vast palette of moods and genres, resulting in music that can range from satisfactory to excellent.

Versatility: The wide range of moods and genres available makes Beethoven.ai a versatile tool for various content creators, catering to all tastes.

Quality: The quality of music generated is variable, indicating potential for excellence alongside the need for occasional user guidance.

Mubert:

Mubert is tailored to generate music for video content, podcasts, and apps. It produces high-quality output, though users may encounter challenges in fine-tuning the results to match their specific visions.

Application: Mubert is a strong choice for content creators looking for background music that enhances their projects, like a musical sidekick.

Precision: While the quality is high, achieving precise musical results may require additional development.

Soundraw.io:

Soundraw.io is your musical library of AI-generated tracks. It offers a collection of tunes for various applications, perfect for when you need the right mood music on demand.

Function: It serves users looking for a wide selection of music that can be quickly and easily applied to their projects.

Selection: The platform provides a broad library, though it differs from other tools that focus on generating music from user-provided inputs..

Aiva.ai:

Aiva.ai is your emotional composer, specializing in creating soundtracks that tug at the heartstrings. With a range of templates and customization options, it offers the feel of royalty-free tracks while maintaining a level of quality that users find satisfactory.

Emotional Intelligence: Aiva.ai excels in understanding the emotional weight of music, crucial for soundtracks that must carry the narrative and emotional undercurrents of visual media, like having a composer who can read your mind.

Customization and Templates: With a variety of templates at your disposal, Aiva.ai provides a starting point that can be molded and shaped to fit the desired emotional tone, making it a flexible tool for composers and filmmakers alike, like having a musical collaborator who speaks your language.

Output Quality. While the music produced by Aiva.ai can sometimes bear the hallmarks of royalty-free tracks, its quality is generally good, and the compositions are emotionally resonant, offering a solid choice for those in need of quick and effective musical scores, like having your own personal maestro.

In the world of AI music creation, these platforms are the virtuosos, each offering its unique sound to help you compose the melody of your dreams. So, whether you're a musical maestro or just starting your composition ride, there's an AI platform waiting to help you create your symphony.

In the ever-evolving world of AI music creation, the platforms we've explored here are just a few notes in a vast symphony of possibilities. There are multiple software solutions out there, each with its own unique melody, waiting for you to discover and experiment with.

So, if you find yourself inspired to venture into the world of AI-generated music, I encourage you to take that first step. Test out these platforms, delve into their capabilities, and let your creativity flow freely. The symphony of AI music creation is yours to compose, and who knows, you may stumble upon the perfect harmonies that bring your musical visions to life.

DATA ANALYSIS WITH GENERATIVE AI

Data analysis has become the lifeblood of decision-making in today's information-driven world. From understanding customer behavior to predicting financial market trends, the ability to extract meaningful insights from data is crucial.

In this chapter, we will explore the fascinating world of data analysis with generative AI. While the previous chapters uncovered how AI can generate text, images, music, and videos, we will now delve into how it can assist in deriving patterns, making predictions, and enhancing decision-making by harnessing the power of generative models.

Data analysis is often a complex and time-consuming process, requiring skilled data scientists to navigate vast datasets, identify trends, and extract valuable insights. Generative AI, with its ability to generate synthetic data, augment existing datasets, and uncover hidden patterns, has emerged as a game-changer in this field.

Generative models such as GANs (Generative Adversarial Networks) and VAEs (Variational Autoencoders) have opened up new possibilities for data analysis. They can generate synthetic data that mirrors real-world distributions, improving the robustness of machine learning models. These models are not just tools for data augmentation but also capable of anomaly detection, data imputation, and even forecasting in the realm of time series data.

The applications of generative AI in data analysis are vast. It extends to natural language processing, enabling sentiment analysis, text summarization, and content recommendation. It encompasses visualization and interpretability, where generative models help turn complex data into understandable visual representations.

In this chapter, we will not only discuss the concepts and principles of data analysis with generative AI but also introduce you to software tools and platforms that make these tasks more accessible than ever before. Whether you are a data scientist looking to enhance your analytical capabilities or a newcomer interested in the fascinating intersection of data and AI, this chapter will provide valuable insights into the evolving landscape of data analysis with generative AI.

Data Augmentation with Generative AI

In the realm of machine learning, the quality and quantity of training data can significantly impact the performance of models. Data augmentation is a technique used to enhance datasets by creating additional data points that maintain the underlying characteristics of the original dataset. Generative AI has emerged as a powerful ally in this endeavor, revolutionizing the process of data augmentation.

Enhancing Dataset Robustness:

Data augmentation with generative AI is akin to having an artist who can craft new data instances while preserving the essence of the original dataset. It involves generating synthetic data points that closely resemble real-world samples, effectively expanding the dataset's size and diversity.

Improving Model Performance:

By introducing variations and novel examples, generative AI-driven data augmentation equips machine learning models with a richer understanding of the data distribution. This not only enhances model generalization but also mitigates overfitting, a common challenge in machine learning.

Examples of Synthetic Data Generation:

Let's consider a few scenarios where generative AI powered data augmentation can work wonders:

1. **Image Recognition**: In a dataset for image recognition, generative AI can create new images by applying transformations such as rotation, scaling, and mirroring to existing images. This expands the dataset's diversity and ensures that the model is robust to variations in real-world images.
2. **Text Classification**: When dealing with text data, generative AI can be used to generate paraphrased sentences or sentences with similar

meanings. This augments the text dataset and helps the model better understand the nuances of language.
3. **Medical Imaging**: In the domain of medical imaging, synthetic images of organs or anomalies can be generated to supplement a limited dataset. This aids in training robust models for disease detection.
4. **Speech Recognition**: For speech recognition tasks, generative AI can create synthetic audio samples by altering pitch, speed, or background noise. This expands the training data and improves the model's ability to recognize diverse speech patterns.
5. **Natural Language Generation**: In tasks like language generation, generative AI can create additional text samples with varying styles, tones, or content. This makes the language model more versatile in generating human-like text.

In each of these examples, generative AI acts as an invaluable tool for expanding datasets, addressing data scarcity issues, and enhancing the overall performance of machine learning models.

Data augmentation powered by generative AI is not just about increasing dataset size; it's about enriching the dataset's quality and diversity.

Anomaly Detection with Generative AI

In the land of data analysis and quality control, identifying anomalies or outliers within datasets is a critical task. Anomalies can signify fraudulent activities, manufacturing defects, or unusual events that require immediate attention. Generative AI has emerged as a potent tool in the domain of anomaly detection, offering the ability to distinguish the ordinary from the extraordinary.

Crucial for Fraud Detection and Quality Control:

Anomaly detection using generative AI is comparable to having a vigilant sentry that tirelessly scans through data, pinpointing irregularities that might go unnoticed through traditional methods. It plays a pivotal role in various domains:

Fraud Detection: In the financial sector, generative AI models can detect unusual patterns in transactions, identifying potential fraud or cyberattacks. Whether it's detecting unauthorized access to accounts or spotting irregular spending behavior, generative AI can act as a guardian against financial threats.

Quality Control: In manufacturing and production, anomalies can lead to defects and inefficiencies. Generative AI can inspect data from sensors, cameras, or sensors to identify deviations from normal operating conditions. This ensures that products meet quality standards, reducing waste and production costs.

Healthcare: In healthcare, anomaly detection can be a lifesaver. Generative AI can analyze patient data, detecting unusual vital signs or medical records that may indicate health issues or potential diseases. This enables early intervention and better patient care.

Software Tools Specializing in Anomaly Detection:

Generative AI-powered anomaly detection is a sophisticated field, and several software tools have emerged to tackle this challenge effectively. Here are some notable examples:

1. **PyOD (Python Outlier Detection)**: PyOD is a comprehensive Python library dedicated to various anomaly detection techniques, including generative models. It offers a wide range of algorithms, making it a versatile choice for data analysts and machine learning practitioners.
2. **H2O.ai**: H2O.ai provides an enterprise-level platform for machine learning and artificial intelligence, including robust anomaly detection capabilities. It utilizes generative models and deep learning techniques to identify anomalies in real-time data streams.
3. **Scikit-learn**: Scikit-learn, a popular machine learning library, offers anomaly detection algorithms suitable for various applications. While not solely focused on generative AI, it provides a good starting point for implementing anomaly detection solutions.
4. **RapidMiner**: RapidMiner is an integrated data science platform that includes anomaly detection capabilities. It employs generative models and machine learning techniques to uncover anomalies in datasets across different industries.
5. **Amazon SageMaker**: Amazon SageMaker offers a cloud-based platform with built-in anomaly detection features. It leverages generative models and machine learning algorithms to identify outliers in diverse datasets.

   These software tools, equipped with generative AI capabilities, empower businesses and organizations to detect anomalies efficiently and proactively respond to unusual occurrences. They serve as essential components in safeguarding financial systems, ensuring product quality, and enhancing overall data-driven decision-making.

Generative AI-driven anomaly detection is not just about identifying deviations from the norm; it's about providing organizations with the insights needed to maintain integrity, security, and quality in their operations.

Data Imputation with Generative AI

Missing data is a common challenge in various industries, and incomplete datasets can hinder accurate analysis and decision-making. Generative AI, with its ability to understand underlying patterns and generate data that fits within those patterns, has emerged as a powerful solution for filling in missing data points. This process, known as data imputation, enhances the completeness of datasets and unlocks new possibilities for analysis.

Enhancing the Completeness of Datasets:

Data imputation using generative AI is like having a skilled puzzle solver who can seamlessly complete missing pieces in a jigsaw. It involves predicting and generating values for missing data points based on the information available in the dataset. This transforms fragmented data into a cohesive and analyzable whole.

Applications in Healthcare, Finance, and Beyond:

Data imputation powered by generative AI finds applications in diverse industries, with healthcare and finance being just the tip of the iceberg:

1. **Healthcare**: In the healthcare sector, patient data often contains gaps due to various reasons, such as missed measurements or incomplete medical records. Generative AI can impute missing medical values, enabling more accurate patient profiling, treatment planning, and research. For example, it can predict missing vital sign measurements, laboratory results, or patient histories, leading to better-informed medical decisions.
2. **Finance**: In the financial world, missing data can lead to inaccurate risk assessments, investment decisions, and fraud detection. Generative AI can help by filling in missing financial transaction data, credit scores, or economic indicators. This improves the accuracy of financial models, aids in detecting anomalies, and enhances fraud prevention systems.
3. **Retail**: In the retail industry, understanding customer behavior is crucial for optimizing sales and marketing strategies. Generative AI can

impute missing customer purchase history, demographic information, or product preferences. This allows retailers to create more personalized customer experiences and targeted marketing campaigns.
4. **Manufacturing**: In manufacturing, missing sensor data or quality control measurements can disrupt production processes and lead to defects. Generative AI can predict missing values in real-time, ensuring smooth operations and maintaining product quality.
5. **Energy**: In the energy sector, missing data in energy consumption patterns or equipment performance can impact efficiency and maintenance schedules. Generative AI can estimate missing values to optimize energy usage, predict equipment failures, and reduce downtime.
6. **Education**: In education, imputing missing student performance data or demographic information can help institutions identify at-risk students and tailor educational programs accordingly.

Generative AI-powered data imputation transcends industry boundaries, providing organizations with more complete and reliable datasets. It enables data-driven decision-making, enhances predictive models, and contributes to better insights across various domains.

Time Series Analysis with Generative AI

Time series data is a series of numbers that tells a story over time, like stock prices or weather measurements. Generative AI helps us understand this story and even predict what might happen next.

The Role of Generative Models in Forecasting and Generating Time Series Data

Generative AI does two main things:

Forecasting the Future: Think of it like a weather forecaster. It looks at past temperatures, for example, and guesses what the temperature might be tomorrow based on those patterns. This is super helpful for making predictions, like if a stock price will go up or down.

Creating New Data: Sometimes, we need more data to test our ideas or improve our models. Generative AI can make new data points that fit the patterns it has learned. For instance, it can create realistic stock prices for days we don't have data for.

Case Studies Where Generative AI Has Improved Predictive Analytics:

Let's look at some real-world examples:

Financial Markets: Generative AI helps investors predict market trends by analyzing historical stock prices. This is crucial for making smart investment choices.

Healthcare: In healthcare, it can predict health issues early by analyzing patient data, saving lives by spotting problems before they get serious.

Energy Consumption: Energy companies use it to forecast electricity demand accurately, reducing costs and being more eco-friendly.

Retail Sales: Retailers predict future sales based on past buying patterns, so they know what to stock and what to recommend to customers.

Weather Forecasting: Generative AI helps us know if it's going to rain tomorrow by learning from past weather data.

Traffic Flow: It helps us avoid traffic jams by analyzing traffic data and suggesting better routes.

Generative AI is like a time-traveler through data, helping us peek into the future by learning from the past. It's not magic, but it's a super-smart tool that helps us make better decisions based on patterns in time series data.

Natural Language Processing for Data Analysis

Text data is a goldmine of information, but it's often unstructured and challenging to decipher. Enter generative AI, a powerful tool that can not only understand and analyze text data but also extract valuable insights and sentiments hidden within the words.

How Generative AI Processes and Analyzes Unstructured Text Data

Generative AI in natural language processing (NLP) is like having a language expert at your service. Here's what it does:

Text Understanding: Generative AI can read and understand text. It knows how words fit together in sentences and understands the nuances of language, like distinguishing between "happy" and "joyful."

Sentiment Analysis: It can figure out how people feel by analyzing text. For example, if someone writes, "I loved the movie!" generative AI recognizes the positive sentiment. This capability is invaluable for understanding customer opinions, brand perception, and market trends.

Extracting Insights: Generative AI can identify essential information within text data. It can automatically find key topics in a lengthy document, summarize articles, and extract structured data from unstructured text.

Language Translation: It's like having an instant translator. Generative AI can translate text from one language to another accurately, facilitating cross-cultural communication and expanding global reach.

Software Tools for Text Analytics Powered by Generative Models:

Let's explore some software tools that leverage generative AI for text analytics:

- **GPT (OpenAI's Generative Pre-trained Transformer):** GPT is a superstar in NLP. It's incredibly versatile, capable of answering questions, generating text, translating languages, and even writing code. It's as if you have a multi-talented language genius at your fingertips.
- **BERT (Bidirectional Encoder Representations from Transformers):** BERT is a sophisticated text analysis tool that excels at understanding context within language. It's especially valuable for tasks like sentiment analysis and grasping the subtleties of textual meaning.
- **NLTK (Natural Language Toolkit):** NLTK is a beginner-friendly Python library for text analysis. It provides various tools and resources for tasks like tokenization, stemming, tagging, parsing, and more.
- **TextBlob:** Another Python library, TextBlob simplifies common NLP tasks, including sentiment analysis, language translation, and part-of-speech tagging. It's known for its user-friendly interface and ease of use.
- **SpaCy:** SpaCy is a highly efficient and accurate NLP library for text analysis. It's suitable for professionals and offers features like tokenization, named entity recognition, and part-of-speech tagging
- **IBM Watson NLU (Natural Language Understanding):** Watson NLU is a robust platform that employs generative AI to analyze text data. It can uncover sentiments, emotions, entities, and more, functioning as a digital analyst that reads and interprets text data comprehensively.

Generative AI in NLP revolutionizes data analysis, enabling organizations to unlock the wealth of information hidden in text. It empowers businesses to understand customer feedback, gain insights from textual data, analyze market trends, and make data-driven decisions with confidence.

CODING WITH AI

In the vast and often bewildering jungle of software development, where the underbrush of syntax errors can trip up even the most seasoned explorers and the quicksand of debugging can suck hours from your day, there emerges a beacon of hope: ChatGPT. This isn't your average, everyday AI; think of it more as the Swiss Army knife in your coding backpack, the trusty compass guiding you through uncharted territories of code.

Imagine, if you will, a world where your coding assistant doesn't just spit out lines of code but does so with the finesse of a seasoned guide, helping you navigate through the dense foliage of programming challenges. That's ChatGPT for you. It's like having a coding buddy who's always there, ready to lend a hand or a snippet, without ever judging your recursive functions or your overuse of global variables.

Developed by the sorcerers over at OpenAI, ChatGPT has quickly become the go-to for developers seeking a less solitary coding experience. It's adept at a range of tasks, from conjuring up code snippets that make you nod in approval to embarking on debugging adventures that feel more like a collaborative puzzle-solving session than a solo slog.

But what sets ChatGPT apart in the coding ecosystem? For starters, it's akin to having a conversation with a fellow developer who's infinitely patient and incredibly knowledgeable, yet never too busy to help. Whether you're a newbie trying to decipher the arcane spells of code or a seasoned developer looking for a fresh perspective, ChatGPT is there to light up the path with its insights.

Understanding ChatGPT's Capabilities in Coding

Advancing into the digital expanse of software development with ChatGPT as our guide, it's essential to understand the breadth and depth of its capabilities. ChatGPT, with its foundation in the latest advancements in artificial intelligence, is not just a tool but a versatile companion for developers. Its prowess spans across a multitude of programming languages and a wide array of coding tasks, making it an indispensable asset in the coder's toolkit.

Language Support

ChatGPT's linguistic dexterity is not confined to human languages alone; its fluency extends into programming languages, making it a polyglot of the coding world. From the foundational C and Java to the modern Python and JavaScript, and even the niche languages like Rust and Go, ChatGPT's support is extensive. Its versatility shines as it seamlessly switches contexts, understanding the syntax, semantics, and idiosyncrasies of each language. Whether you're working on a web development project in HTML and CSS, crafting complex data analysis scripts in Python, or venturing into the concurrency of Go, ChatGPT stands ready to assist.

Task Range

The capabilities of ChatGPT in coding are as varied as the landscape of software development itself. Here's a glimpse into the range of tasks it can help with:

- **Code Generation**: At the heart of ChatGPT's utility is its ability to generate code snippets. Whether you need a quick function in Python to parse JSON data or a complex SQL query to extract insights from a database, ChatGPT can generate these on the fly, tailored to your specifications.

- **Debugging Assistance**: One of the most time-consuming aspects of coding is debugging. ChatGPT can help identify logical errors, syntax mistakes, and other common bugs. By analyzing the code and the error messages, it can suggest potential fixes or guide you through the debugging process step by step.

- **Explaining Complex Algorithms**: Algorithms are the building blocks of programming, but understanding them can sometimes be daunting. ChatGPT can break down complex algorithms into simpler, understandable components. Whether it's explaining the intricacies of sorting algorithms like QuickSort or demystifying data structures like binary trees, ChatGPT can make learning these concepts more accessible.

- **Code Reviews**: ChatGPT can assist in reviewing code by providing insights on best practices, potential inefficiencies, and areas for improvement. It can suggest more optimal ways to structure code, enhance readability, and ensure maintainability.

- **Learning and Mentorship**: For those new to coding or looking to expand their skill set, ChatGPT can serve as a mentor. It can provide explanations, examples, and resources tailored to the learner's pace and level of understanding, making the progress path into coding less intimidating and more engaging.

- **Integration and API Usage**: In today's interconnected digital world, understanding how to integrate and use APIs is crucial. ChatGPT can guide developers through the process of integrating third-party services and APIs into their projects, providing examples of API calls and explaining the responses.

In essence, ChatGPT's capabilities in coding extend far beyond mere code generation. Its ability to assist with a wide range of coding tasks, coupled with its support for numerous programming languages, positions it as a valuable ally in the quest to navigate the complexities of software development.

How ChatGPT Enhances Coding Productivity

In the dynamic world of software development, productivity is not just about writing code faster; it's about writing smarter code, debugging efficiently, and optimizing for performance and readability. ChatGPT emerges as a catalyst in this, significantly enhancing coding productivity through its AI-driven capabilities. Let's explore how ChatGPT accomplishes this feat across code generation, debugging assistance, and code optimization.

Code Generation

ChatGPT's ability to generate code based on user prompts is akin to having a co-pilot in the coding process. This feature is particularly beneficial for both rapid prototyping and implementing complex functionalities.

- **Simple Scripts**: For instance, if you need a quick Python script to scrape data from a webpage, you might prompt ChatGPT with, "Generate a Python script to scrape titles from a webpage using BeautifulSoup." ChatGPT can then provide a concise script, complete with necessary imports, function definitions, and error handling, saving you the initial research and setup time.
- **Complex Functions**: On a more complex note, consider requiring a function to implement a specific sorting algorithm with custom sorting criteria. A prompt like, "Write a JavaScript function to sort an array of objects by a 'date' property using the Merge Sort algorithm" would result in ChatGPT generating a tailored function. This not only aids in accomplishing the task at hand but also serves as an educational tool, demonstrating the implementation of algorithms in a practical context.

Debugging Assistance

Debugging is often where most time is spent in the development cycle. ChatGPT's prowess in identifying and suggesting fixes for errors can significantly reduce this time.

- **Syntax Errors**: ChatGPT can easily spot syntax errors that might elude developers, especially in verbose languages. For example, if a piece of code fails due to a missing semicolon in JavaScript, ChatGPT can pinpoint the exact line and suggest the addition, turning a potentially frustrating search into a quick fix.

- **Logical Errors**: More impressively, ChatGPT can assist with logical errors by understanding the intended outcome described by the user. If a function is supposed to return the nth Fibonacci number but instead enters an infinite loop, ChatGPT can analyze the code, identify the logical flaw, and propose a corrected version of the function, often elucidating the reasoning behind the error.

Code Optimization

Beyond generating and debugging code, ChatGPT can guide developers in refining their code for better efficiency and readability.

- **Performance Enhancements**: ChatGPT can suggest algorithmic improvements or highlight inefficient code patterns. For example, if a piece of code iterates over a large dataset multiple times unnecessarily, ChatGPT might suggest a more efficient algorithmic approach, such as using hash maps for faster lookups, thereby improving the overall performance.

- **Readability and Best Practices**: ChatGPT can also recommend changes to enhance code readability, adhering to best practices. It might suggest breaking down a complex, nested function into smaller, more manageable functions or adopting naming conventions that make the code more understandable at a glance.

In essence, ChatGPT acts as a multifaceted tool in a developer's arsenal, not just accelerating the coding process but also elevating the quality of the output. By assisting with code generation, offering debugging support, and guiding code optimization, ChatGPT not only enhances productivity but also fosters a deeper understanding of coding principles, ultimately leading to the development of better software.

CHATGPT IN EVERYDAY LIFE: YOUR AI ASSISTANT

In the rapidly evolving landscape of artificial intelligence, ChatGPT stands out as a versatile and powerful tool, extending its utility far beyond simple text generation. As an AI assistant, ChatGPT can simplify, enhance, and add efficiency to various aspects of everyday life. This chapter delves into how ChatGPT can be seamlessly integrated into daily routines, serving as a personal assistant that offers support across a myriad of tasks.

SIMPLIFYING COMMUNICATION

Emails and Correspondence: Drafting emails can be time-consuming, especially when trying to convey the right tone. ChatGPT can assist by generating professional, polite, or casual email drafts based on your brief inputs, ensuring you communicate effectively without spending too much time staring at a blank screen.

Language Translation and Learning: Whether you're learning a new language or need to translate text, ChatGPT can provide translations and explanations, making it easier to understand foreign documents or communicate with speakers of other languages.

ENHANCING PRODUCTIVITY

Task Management: ChatGPT can help organize your tasks and to-do lists, offering suggestions for prioritizing work and setting reminders. It can act as a virtual project manager, helping you keep track of deadlines and deliverables.

Research Assistance: From academic research to casual curiosity, ChatGPT can summarize articles, explain complex concepts, and offer insights on a wide range of topics, significantly cutting down the time you spend digging through search engine results.

Creative Endeavors

Writing and Content Creation: Whether you're experiencing writer's block or need inspiration for your next blog post, ChatGPT can generate ideas, outlines, or even complete drafts, sparking creativity and helping to refine your narrative.

Cooking and Recipes: ChatGPT can suggest recipes based on the ingredients you have, provide step-by-step cooking instructions, or even offer ideas for meal planning, making it easier to answer the perennial question, "What's for dinner?"

LEARNING AND DEVELOPMENT

Educational Support: Students can use ChatGPT to understand difficult subjects, generate practice questions, and receive explanations for various topics, making learning more interactive and engaging.

Skill Acquisition: Interested in picking up a new hobby or skill? ChatGPT can guide you through the basics of anything from coding to knitting, offering resources, tutorials, and tips to get you started.

DAILY DECISION MAKING

Travel Planning: ChatGPT can assist in planning your next vacation, offering travel tips, suggesting destinations based on your preferences, and even helping to create an itinerary that matches your interests and budget.

Shopping and Fashion Advice: Whether you're looking for the best deal on a new gadget or need advice on what to wear for an upcoming event, ChatGPT can provide recommendations, compare products, and offer styling tips.

PERSONAL WELL-BEING

Mental Health Support: While not a substitute for professional care, ChatGPT can offer mindfulness exercises, stress-relief techniques, and motivational quotes to help users navigate challenging times with a bit of comfort.

Fitness Coaching: ChatGPT can suggest workout routines, track fitness progress, and offer nutritional advice, acting as a virtual fitness coach to help you achieve your health goals.

ChatGPT's integration into everyday life signifies a leap towards a future where AI assists in bridging the gap between human intention and action. By leveraging this powerful tool, individuals can unlock new levels of efficiency, creativity, and personal growth. As we continue to explore and expand the capabilities of AI like ChatGPT, the potential for transformative impacts on daily life becomes increasingly apparent, making it an indispensable assistant for a wide range of tasks.

THE CRAFT OF PROMPT ENGINEERING WITH CHATGPT

Prompt engineering is a nuanced art form that requires a blend of precision, understanding, and creativity, similar to a conversation with a highly intelligent machine, where the clarity and structure of your questions dictate the quality and relevance of the responses you receive. This chapter takes a closer look at how to master this craft, applying it to everyday tasks to unlock the full potential of ChatGPT as an AI assistant.

UNDERSTANDING THE BASICS OF EFFECTIVE PROMPTING

Clarity and Specificity: The essence of an effective prompt lies in its clarity. Like providing directions to a traveler, the more detailed and clear your instructions, the less likely they are to get lost. Specify exactly what you need from ChatGPT to ensure the output aligns with your expectations.

Contextual Depth: Adding context to your prompts is like setting the scene before the main act of a play. It gives ChatGPT the background information needed to tailor its responses more accurately to your query, enhancing the relevance of the output.

Iterative Refinement: Crafting the perfect prompt is often a process of trial and error. Each interaction with ChatGPT is an opportunity to refine your approach, gradually honing in on the language and structure that yield the best results.

ADVANCED TECHNIQUES IN PROMPT ENGINEERING

Zero-shot, Few-shot, and Many-shot Learning: These approaches vary in the amount of guidance you provide. From giving no examples (zero-shot) to providing several (many-shot), each technique has its place, depending on the complexity of the task and the specificity of the desired output.

Chain of Thought Prompting: Leading ChatGPT through a logical sequence of thoughts or steps can be particularly effective for complex problem-solving. It's about breaking down the process into manageable chunks that the AI can follow.

Instruction Following: Direct and straightforward instructions can significantly improve the utility of ChatGPT's responses. It's about being explicit in what you're asking for, whether it's a summary, an analysis, or creative content.

REAL-WORLD APPLICATIONS OF PROMPT ENGINEERING

Content Creation: From drafting articles to generating creative stories, the right prompts can turn ChatGPT into a prolific creator, offering fresh perspectives and ideas that can spark your own creativity.

Data Analysis and Interpretation: ChatGPT can assist in making sense of data, providing summaries, insights, and even visualizations, provided you guide it with clear, structured prompts.

Educational Support: Whether it's explaining complex concepts in simpler terms or providing practice problems, effective prompt engineering can make ChatGPT an invaluable learning aid.

Customer Service: Tailored prompts can transform ChatGPT into a responsive and helpful customer service assistant, capable of addressing inquiries and providing solutions in a conversational manner.

BEST PRACTICES IN PROMPT ENGINEERING

Experimentation: The key to mastering prompt engineering is willingness to experiment. Each interaction with ChatGPT is an opportunity to learn what works best, adapting your approach as you go.

Community Learning: Engaging with the wider community of ChatGPT users can offer new insights and strategies for prompt engineering, helping you avoid common pitfalls and discover innovative approaches.

Staying Informed: The field of AI is rapidly evolving. Keeping abreast of the latest developments can provide you with new tools and techniques to enhance your prompt engineering skills.

To summarize, to create an effective prompt that elicits the desired response from ChatGPT, consider the following advice:

1. **Be Clear and Specific**: Ensure your prompt is direct and detailed. Avoid vagueness to minimize the risk of irrelevant or broad answers.
2. **Incorporate Context**: Provide sufficient background information to guide the AI's response, especially for complex or nuanced queries.

3. **Use Iterative Refinement**: View prompt crafting as a process. Based on the AI's responses, refine your prompts to improve accuracy and relevance.

4. **Apply Learning Techniques**: Depending on the task, use zero-shot (no examples), few-shot (a few examples), or many-shot (many examples) learning to guide the AI.

5. **Guide with Chain of Thought**: For complex problems, break down the process into steps within your prompt, leading the AI through the reasoning process.

6. **Be Direct with Instructions**: State explicitly what you expect in the response, whether it's an analysis, a summary, or creative content.

7. **Anticipate AI Limitations**: Understand that AI may not grasp ambiguity or nuance the same way humans do. Anticipate where misunderstandings could occur and structure your prompt to preclude them.

8. **Set the Tone**: If you want the AI to generate content in a particular voice or style, specify this in your prompt. For example, if you want a professional report, mention that; if you're looking for a humorous blog post, make that clear.

9. **Ask for Examples**: If you're using AI to generate ideas or need examples for clarification, ask for them directly. For example, "Provide three examples of how to reduce water waste at home."

10. **Limit Scope**: If you're looking for a concise answer, set parameters for the AI. You can limit the number of bullet points, word count, or ask for a one-sentence summary to keep responses focused.

11. **Sequence Your Questions**: If you have multiple questions, consider breaking them up into separate prompts. This can prevent overwhelming the AI and ensure each question is addressed adequately.

12. **Use Keywords**: Incorporate relevant keywords in your prompts to help the AI understand the topic's context and relevance better.

13. **Feedback Loop**: Use the AI's responses as feedback. If the output isn't what you expected, adjust your prompt accordingly and

consider providing feedback to the AI about why the response didn't meet your needs.
14. **Be Creative**: Don't be afraid to experiment with different types of prompts. Creative questioning can sometimes lead to unexpectedly useful and innovative responses.
15. **Leverage Suggestions**: If the AI offers suggestions or asks clarifying questions, use them to refine your prompt further. This can lead to a more targeted and effective interaction.

Bad Prompt for Improving Productivity

"Tell me how to do better at work."

Why It's Ineffective:

- It's vague and does not specify what "do better" means.
- There is no context provided about the nature of the work, the current productivity challenges, or the working environment.
- It doesn't guide the AI with a specific task or format for the response.
- It does not set a tone, ask for examples, or use keywords that could help tailor the response.

Good Prompt for Improving Productivity

"I work from home as a software developer and recently have been struggling to meet project deadlines, which I suspect is due to frequent distractions and poor time management. Could you provide a structured plan with five detailed strategies to enhance my productivity? Please include techniques for minimizing distractions, effective time management methods, and tools that could assist in keeping me focused on work tasks. Additionally, suggest how I might incorporate these strategies into a daily routine, and offer examples of apps or methods that have proven successful for others in similar roles."

Why It's Effective:

- The prompt is clear and specific about the issue: improving productivity in meeting project deadlines.
- It provides context about the user's job, working environment, and suspected productivity challenges.

- It indicates a desire for iterative refinement by asking for a structured plan, implying the possibility of follow-up questions.
- It asks for examples (apps or methods) and specifies a format for the response (a plan with five strategies).
- It anticipates AI limitations by clarifying the nature of the work and the specific problems faced.
- The tone is set to be solution-focused and practical.
- It sequences the request: first, strategies; then, incorporation into a routine; and finally, examples for application.
- It uses keywords relevant to the user's situation: software developer, distractions, time management, project deadlines.
- It establishes a feedback loop by providing a base for further refinement of the strategies suggested.

In the ever-evolving landscape of artificial intelligence, prompt engineering emerges as an artful craft, akin to having a meaningful conversation with a highly intelligent machine. It's a craft that requires precision, understanding, and creativity, where the quality of the responses you receive hinges on the clarity and structure of your questions.

CUSTOM INSTRUCTIONS IN CHAT GBT

Using the custom instruction feature in ChatGPT allows users to personalize their interaction with the AI, tailoring responses to fit specific needs, preferences, or contexts. This feature is particularly useful for setting a default behavior or providing background information that influences how ChatGPT generates its responses. Here's a step-by-step guide on how to use the custom instruction feature in ChatGPT:

1. Accessing Custom Instructions

- **Open ChatGPT**: Log in to your ChatGPT account.
- **Navigate to Settings**: In the ChatGPT interface, look for a settings icon or your profile icon, usually found in the bottom left corner or the sidebar menu.
- **Select Custom Instructions**: Within the settings or profile menu, find and click on the option labeled "Custom Instructions" or something similar.

2. Setting Up Custom Instructions

- **Provide Information About You**: In the first text box, you're encouraged to input details about yourself that you want ChatGPT to consider when generating responses. This could include your profession, interests, location, or any other relevant information that could influence the AI's responses.

Example: "I'm a web developer specializing in front-end technologies. I enjoy reading about space exploration and have a keen interest in sustainable living practices."

- **Specify Response Preferences**: In the second text box, describe how you'd like ChatGPT to respond. This can include the tone of the responses (formal, casual, humorous, etc.), the format (bullet points, concise answers, detailed explanations), and any other preferences regarding the content or style of the responses.

Example: "Please provide responses in a concise, bullet-point format whenever possible. Use a friendly tone but keep the explanations professional. Avoid using technical jargon without explanations."

3. Enabling Custom Instructions

- **Save Your Settings**: After filling out the information and response preferences, look for a save or apply button to save your custom instructions.
- **Enable for New Chats**: Ensure there's an option or a toggle to apply these custom instructions to all new chat sessions. Enable it if you want your custom instructions to be automatically applied to every new chat.

4. Using Custom Instructions in Chats

- **Start a New Chat**: Begin a new chat session with ChatGPT.
- **Observe the Impact**: Notice how ChatGPT incorporates your custom instructions into its responses. It should take into account the information about you and adhere to your specified response preferences.

5. Adjusting Custom Instructions

- **Review and Refine**: After using ChatGPT with your custom instructions, you might find areas for adjustment. Perhaps you want to change the tone, add more details about your interests, or specify different response formats for certain types of inquiries.

- **Update Instructions**: Return to the custom instructions setting to make any adjustments. Update your preferences and save the changes to refine how ChatGPT interacts with you.

Tips for Effective Custom Instructions

- **Be Specific**: The more specific you are in your instructions, the more tailored and relevant ChatGPT's responses will be.
- **Experiment**: Don't hesitate to experiment with different instructions to find what works best for your needs.
- **Update Regularly**: As your needs or interests change, update your custom instructions to reflect these changes, ensuring ChatGPT remains a valuable tool for you.

Custom instructions in ChatGPT offer a powerful way to personalize your AI interactions, making the tool more aligned with your specific needs and preferences. By following these steps and tips, you can enhance your ChatGPT experience, making it more efficient and enjoyable.

FUTURE OF GENERATIVE AI

As we stand on the precipice of a new era in technology, Generative AI emerges as a beacon of innovation, illuminating the path forward with its remarkable capabilities. This branch of artificial intelligence, known for its ability to create new, original content that mimics real-world data, has already begun to reshape the rules of numerous fields, from art and design to science and engineering. It's as if we've unlocked a new dimension of creativity and problem-solving, one where the lines between human and machine-generated content blur, offering a glimpse into a future brimming with possibilities.

Generative AI, the cool creator of the AI family, has evolved from playing games of chess to writing the rules for entirely new games. It represents a shift from AI systems that interpret and respond to data, to those that can imagine and create, producing everything from photorealistic images to novel drug compounds. This capability to generate diverse and complex outputs, comparable to a novelist who can effortlessly switch between genres, marks a significant leap forward in our path with AI.

The applications of Generative AI are as varied as they are impressive, touching every corner of human endeavor. In art, it challenges our perceptions of creativity and authorship. In science, it accelerates research and discovery, offering solutions to some of the most pressing challenges of our time. In business, it personalizes customer experiences to a degree previously unimaginable, transforming how companies interact with their audiences.

But when venturing deeper into the world of Generative AI, we must also navigate the complexities and challenges that accompany its rise. The ethical considerations, the impact on jobs and privacy, and the sheer computational power required to fuel these AI models are just a few of the hurdles we face. Moreover, as Generative AI continues to evolve, so too will its applications, pushing the boundaries of what we believe to be possible and challenging us to rethink the role of technology in our lives.

This chapter aims to explore the potential future developments of Generative AI, exploring the technological advancements on the horizon, the expanding applications across various domains, and the societal impacts of this transformative technology. We will examine the challenges and ethical considerations that lie ahead, and speculate on the innovations that could redefine our relationship with AI.

INCREASED MODEL EFFICIENCY IN GENERATIVE AI

The quest for increased model efficiency in Generative AI is a pivotal area of advancement, addressing the dual challenges of escalating computational demands and environmental sustainability. As Generative AI models delve into more complex and creative tasks, the imperative for efficiency becomes even more pronounced. Let's delve deeper into the innovations driving this pursuit of efficiency.

Advancements in Lightweight Models

The development of lightweight models represents a significant stride towards democratizing Generative AI. These models are designed to deliver high performance without the hefty computational load traditionally associated with AI tasks.

- **Architectural Innovations**: New architectures are being explored that optimize the flow of data through the model, reducing redundancy and enhancing computational efficiency. Techniques like network sparsification, where unnecessary connections within a neural network are eliminated, contribute to creating models that are both lean and potent.

- **Edge AI Integration**: The push towards lightweight models aligns with the growing trend of Edge AI, where AI computations are performed on local devices instead of centralized data centers. This not only reduces latency and bandwidth usage but also opens up new applications for Generative AI in real-time environments, from augmented reality experiences to autonomous vehicle navigation.

Energy-Efficient Computing Practices

As the environmental impact of AI becomes a growing concern, the field is moving towards more sustainable practices. Energy-efficient computing seeks to minimize the carbon footprint of AI operations, making Generative AI more aligned with global sustainability goals.

- **Algorithmic Efficiency**: Beyond hardware innovations, there's a focus on refining algorithms for greater efficiency. Techniques like pruning, which streamlines neural networks by removing non-critical neurons, and quantization, which reduces the precision of the calculations without significantly impacting performance, are key strategies. These methods help in creating models that require less computational power, thereby reducing energy consumption.

- **Knowledge Distillation**: This technique involves transferring the knowledge from a large, complex model to a smaller, more efficient one. The "student" model learns to mimic the "teacher" model's behavior, achieving comparable performance with a fraction of the computational requirements. Knowledge distillation not only makes Generative AI models more energy-efficient but also facilitates their deployment in resource-constrained environments.

The Path to Sustainable AI

The drive towards increased model efficiency and energy-efficient computing is part of a broader movement towards sustainable AI. This includes:

- **Renewable Energy Sources**: Encouraging the use of renewable energy sources for data centers that train and run AI models. By powering AI operations with green energy, the overall environmental impact of these computationally intensive tasks can be significantly reduced.
- **Lifecycle Management**: Considering the entire lifecycle of AI models, from development and training to deployment and decommissioning, with an eye towards sustainability. This holistic approach ensures that every stage is optimized for minimal environmental impact.

The future of Generative AI lies in balancing the scales between computational power and efficiency, creativity and sustainability. As researchers and developers forge ahead, the innovations in lightweight models and energy-efficient computing practices are setting the stage for a new era of Generative AI.

INTEGRATION OF MULTIMODAL MODELS IN GENERATIVE AI

The integration of multimodal models marks a transformative phase in the evolution of Generative AI, pushing the boundaries of how machines understand and interact with the world. By weaving together diverse strands of data—text, images, audio, and video—these models are setting the stage for a future where AI can create and comprehend with a richness and depth akin to human perception.

Seamless Content Creation

The ability of multimodal models to seamlessly blend different types of data opens up unprecedented possibilities for content creation. This integration allows for the generation of complex, multifaceted content that can adapt to various contexts and audiences.

- **Dynamic Media Production**: Imagine an AI system that can produce a complete news report by analyzing written articles, generating relevant imagery, composing background music, and even synthesizing a narrated audio track. Such a system could tailor its output to the preferences of individual users, changing the tone, style, or depth of information based on user interaction.

- **Interactive Experiences**: Multimodal Generative AI can also revolutionize interactive media, such as video games and virtual reality. By understanding and generating content across multiple modalities, AI can create dynamic environments that respond to user actions in real-time, offering a level of immersion and personalization previously unattainable.

Enhanced Understanding

The integration of multimodal models goes beyond content creation; it fundamentally enhances AI's understanding of the world. By processing and correlating information from various sources, these models can grasp the subtleties of human communication, context, and sentiment more deeply.

- **Contextual Awareness**: Multimodal models can discern context with remarkable sensitivity, interpreting the interplay between text, visual cues, and tone of voice to understand situations in a way that single-modality models cannot. This could lead to more intuitive digital assistants, capable of understanding requests and emotions with greater nuance.

- **Sentiment and Subtlety**: These models are also advancing in their ability to detect and interpret sentiment and subtleties across different forms of media. For instance, a multimodal AI could analyze a movie scene, understanding the emotional dynamics between characters not just from the dialogue but from facial expressions, body language, and musical score, enabling it to generate reviews or content summaries that capture the essence of the scene.

Future Directions

As multimodal models continue to evolve, we stand on the brink of a new era in AI, one where machines can create and understand with a complexity that mirrors human intelligence.

- **Cross-Modal Learning**: Future advancements may include models that can not only process but also translate between different modalities, such as converting visual scenes into descriptive text or translating spoken words into animated gestures.
- **Ethical and Creative Collaboration**: The rise of multimodal Generative AI also raises questions about ethics and creativity. As these models become more capable of producing human-like content, the lines between AI-generated and human-created work will blur, challenging our notions of authorship and creativity. This calls for a thoughtful approach to collaboration between humans and AI, ensuring that AI serves as a tool for enhancing human creativity rather than replacing it.

The integration of multimodal models represents a leap towards a future where Generative AI can interact with the world in all its complexity, offering new avenues for creativity, understanding, and innovation.

ADVANCES IN PERSONALIZATION THROUGH GENERATIVE AI

The frontier of personalization is being redefined by Generative AI, promising a future where digital experiences are not just tailored to the individual but are also adaptive, evolving in real-time with the user's changing needs and preferences. This leap in personalization capabilities heralds a new era of user experience, deeply integrated with the nuances of human behavior and expectation.

Dynamic Content Generation

Generative AI is poised to transform content creation, making it dynamically responsive to the user's current context, historical preferences, and even future needs. This level of personalization extends across various domains, offering a glimpse into a future where every digital interaction is uniquely tailored.

- **Adaptive Learning Environments**: In education, Generative AI can create personalized learning journeys, adjusting the difficulty level, content format, and pacing in real-time based on the student's performance and engagement. This could revolutionize education, making learning more effective by catering to the unique needs of each learner.

- **Customized Entertainment**: Imagine streaming platforms that not only recommend movies and shows based on your viewing history but also adapt their narratives or presentation styles to match your mood or preferences at any given moment. Generative AI could enable the creation of interactive media that evolves with viewer feedback, offering a truly personalized entertainment experience.

Personalized Digital Interactions

The advancement in Generative AI will usher in a new level of digital interaction, where AI-powered services can understand and anticipate user needs with remarkable accuracy, offering personalized guidance, support, and companionship.

- **Intuitive Digital Assistants**: Future digital assistants powered by Generative AI will go beyond executing simple commands, engaging in meaningful conversations, providing personalized advice, and even anticipating needs before they are articulated. These assistants could manage everything from scheduling to suggesting activities based on the user's interests and historical behavior.

- **Enhanced Customer Service**: Customer service bots will become more sophisticated, capable of handling complex queries with a level of understanding and empathy previously only achievable by human agents. By analyzing a customer's past interactions and preferences, these bots can offer solutions that are not only relevant but also preemptively address potential concerns.

- **Digital Companions**: Generative AI could give rise to digital companions that offer social interaction and support tailored to the user's personality and emotional state. These AI companions could engage in conversations, offer encouragement, or provide company, all while adapting to the user's changing moods and needs.

The Path to Hyper-Personalization

As we move towards this future of enhanced personalization, several considerations will shape the development and deployment of these technologies:

- **Privacy and Trust**: The deep level of personalization offered by Generative AI requires access to a wealth of personal data. Ensuring the privacy and security of this data is paramount, as is building trust with users regarding how their information is used and protected.
- **Ethical Considerations**: The ability of AI to predict and influence user behavior brings ethical considerations to the forefront. Developers and policymakers must navigate these challenges carefully, ensuring that AI-driven personalization enhances user autonomy rather than undermining it.
- **Technological Challenges**: Achieving this level of personalization requires significant advancements in AI's understanding of human behavior, language, and emotion. Ongoing research and development in natural language processing, emotional AI, and behavioral analytics will be key to realizing the full potential of personalized Generative AI.

The future of personalization, powered by Generative AI, promises to transform our digital experiences, making them more responsive, intuitive, and, ultimately, more human.

SOCIETAL IMPACT OF GENERATIVE AI

Impact on Employment and the Workforce

The advent of Generative AI is reshaping the landscape of employment and the workforce in profound ways. As industries across the board begin to harness the power of Generative AI, the ripple effects on jobs, workplace dynamics, and the very nature of work are becoming increasingly apparent. This section delves into the nuances of how Generative AI is influencing employment trends and transforming workplace environments.

Job Creation vs. Displacement

The dual-edged sword of Generative AI brings with it both opportunities for job creation and challenges of job displacement. Understanding and navigating this transition is crucial for ensuring a future where technology and human talent coexist harmoniously.

- **Emerging Job Categories**: Generative AI is at the forefront of creating entirely new job categories, particularly in fields that require human oversight of AI outputs, ethical considerations in AI deployment, and the customization of AI models for specific industry needs. Roles such as AI ethicists, data annotators, and AI integration specialists are becoming increasingly important, highlighting the need for skills that complement AI capabilities.

- **Mitigating Displacement**: While the automation capabilities of Generative AI may render certain tasks and roles obsolete, the focus is shifting towards re-skilling and up-skilling the workforce. Governments, educational institutions, and corporations are recognizing the importance of preparing individuals for the jobs of the future, emphasizing digital literacy, critical thinking, and creativity—skills that AI is unlikely to supplant in the foreseeable future.

Evolving Workplaces: The New Paradigm of Work

Generative AI is not just changing what we work on but also how we work. The integration of AI into workplace tools and processes is fostering more efficient and flexible work environments, challenging traditional notions of productivity and collaboration.

- **Enhanced Productivity and Creativity**: By automating routine and repetitive tasks, Generative AI allows workers to focus on higher-level, creative, and strategic activities. This shift is enabling teams to tackle more complex problems and innovate at a faster pace, driving forward business growth and development.

- **Remote Work and Collaboration**: The capabilities of Generative AI are also facilitating remote work and global collaboration. AI-powered tools can manage schedules, optimize workflows, and even translate languages in real-time, making it easier for distributed teams to work together effectively. This democratization of access to work opportunities is breaking down geographical barriers, creating a more inclusive global workforce.

Preparing for the Future of Work

As we look towards the future, it's clear that the impact of Generative AI on employment and the workforce will continue to evolve. Preparing for this future requires proactive measures from all sectors of society.

- **Policy and Governance**: Governments must play a key role in shaping policies that support workforce transitions, including social safety nets for displaced workers, incentives for businesses to invest in employee re-skilling, and regulations that ensure the ethical use of AI in the workplace.

- **Corporate Responsibility**: Businesses have a responsibility to invest in their employees' future, offering training programs that equip workers with the skills needed in an AI-driven world. Embracing a culture of lifelong learning and adaptability will be key to navigating the changes brought about by Generative AI.
- **Educational Innovation**: The education system must adapt to the changing job landscape, emphasizing skills that will be in demand in an AI-augmented world. This includes not only technical skills related to AI and data science but also soft skills like problem-solving, emotional intelligence, and adaptability.

Ethical and Privacy Concerns in the Age of AI

The ascent of Generative AI into mainstream applications has illuminated a complex web of ethical and privacy concerns. As this technology continues to evolve, it challenges our societal norms, legal frameworks, and ethical boundaries. Delving deeper into these concerns reveals the multifaceted implications of Generative AI and underscores the need for a proactive approach to governance and regulation.

Misinformation and Authenticity

The capacity of Generative AI to produce highly realistic and convincing fake content, known as deepfakes, has emerged as a significant ethical challenge. This technology's potential misuse spans various domains, from politics and news to personal reputation and security, raising critical questions about trust and truth in the digital age.

- **Combatting Deepfakes**: The fight against deepfakes requires a combination of technological solutions, legal measures, and public awareness. AI detection tools that can identify AI-generated content are being developed, but as the technology improves, so does the sophistication of deepfakes. Legal frameworks that penalize the malicious creation and distribution of deepfakes are essential, as is educating the public on the existence and identification of such content.
- **Promoting Digital Literacy**: Enhancing digital literacy is crucial in empowering individuals to critically assess and question the authenticity of digital content. Educational initiatives that teach media literacy, including the understanding of AI-generated content, can help build a more informed and discerning public.

Data Privacy and Security: Safeguarding Personal Information

As Generative AI systems require access to vast datasets to learn and generate content, concerns about data privacy and security become increasingly pertinent. The collection, storage, and use of personal data for AI training pose significant risks if not managed responsibly.

- **Robust Data Protection Laws**: The development and enforcement of comprehensive data protection laws are critical in safeguarding personal information. Regulations like the GDPR in Europe set a precedent for the kind of legal frameworks needed to manage data privacy in the era of AI, requiring consent for data collection, ensuring data minimization, and granting individuals control over their data.
- **Ethical AI Development**: Beyond legal compliance, ethical considerations must guide the development and deployment of Generative AI. This includes transparent data usage policies, ethical review boards for AI projects, and the implementation of privacy-by-design principles, which integrate data protection measures from the outset of AI system development.

Future Directions

Addressing the ethical and privacy concerns associated with Generative AI necessitates a multifaceted approach, involving stakeholders from across the spectrum of society.

- **International Collaboration**: The global nature of digital technology and AI calls for international collaboration in developing standards and regulations that address ethical and privacy concerns. Harmonizing these efforts can help create a cohesive framework that protects individuals' rights and promotes the responsible use of AI.
- **AI Accountability Frameworks**: Developing frameworks for AI accountability that include clear guidelines for ethical AI development, deployment, and use is essential. These frameworks should ensure that AI systems are transparent, explainable, and aligned with societal values and norms.
- **Public Engagement**: Engaging the public in conversations about the ethical use of Generative AI and its societal implications is crucial. Public forums, stakeholder consultations, and participatory design processes can help ensure that AI development is aligned with the public interest.

CONCLUSION

As we turn the final page of our journey through the intricate and fascinating world of Artificial Intelligence and Generative AI, we find ourselves peering into the future—a future as promising and unpredictable as a cat on a Roomba. From the foundational stones of AI to the soaring heights of Generative AI, we've navigated through the worlds of technology, creativity, ethics, and the societal tapestry they weave together.

This narrative isn't just a tale of human ingenuity and the quest for knowledge; it's a sitcom of sorts, where humans and machines come together in an ensemble cast, each episode filled with moments of breakthrough, bafflement, and the occasional facepalm. It's a story that reflects our own evolution, our aspirations to break free from the mundane, and our relentless pursuit of a future that once flickered only in the neon lights of science fiction.

In the world of Generative AI, where machines can paint masterpieces and pen sonnets, we're reminded that the essence of creativity might just be the most human thing about us. Yet, facing challenges like misinformation, job displacement, and ethical conundrums, we're also reminded that navigating the future with AI is as teaching a robot dog new tricks—exciting, a bit unpredictable, but full of potential.

Looking forward, the path with AI is as filled with potential plot twists as a mystery novel written by an algorithm that's a fan of Agatha Christie and Douglas Adams. It's a path of innovation, exploration, and yes, a bit of uncertainty. But it's also a path we tread with optimism, equipped with the knowledge that the future of AI is crafted not just by our technological achievements but by our collective values, ethics, and perhaps most importantly, our sense of humor.

In this future, where AI might compose a symphony one day and accidentally order a hundred pizzas the next, a dash of humor will be our best companion. After all, in a world where AI can generate art, solve complex problems, and maybe even attempt humor, the next big breakthrough might just be an AI that understands the punchline of a joke about itself.

As this exploration concludes, let's not forget that the saga of AI is a human story at its core. It's about how we harness this extraordinary technology to enhance our lives, empower our communities, and navigate the digital age with grace (and maybe a little bit of clumsiness). The future of Generative AI is not etched in silicon but in the choices we make, the policies we advocate for, and the dreams we chase—with a bit of laughter shared along the way.

I hope you found this exploration as enlightening and entertaining as intended. If this book has sparked new ideas, offered insights, or simply brought a smile to your face, I would be deeply grateful if you could share your experience with others.

Leaving a review on Amazon not only helps me understand what resonated with you but also guides others in discovering this book. Your feedback is invaluable, not just for its potential to encourage the curious and the skeptics alike to embark on their own exploration of AI but also for shaping the future narratives I hope to share with you.

Simply scan the QR code above to leave your review on Amazon. Your support means the world to me and to all those who contributed to making this book a reality. Together, let's continue to demystify AI, one page at a time.

Thank you for joining me on this adventure.

Made in the USA
Las Vegas, NV
08 May 2024